HEIRLOOM GIFTS

HEIRLOOM GIFTS

*Handmade gifts
to pass down from
generation to generation*

ANNA GRIFFITHS

a Salamander book

Published by Salamander Books Limited
LONDON

For my family with love

A SALAMANDER BOOK

Published by Salamander Books Ltd,
129-137 York Way,
London N7 9LG,
United Kingdom

Distributed by Random House Value Publishing, Inc.
40 Engelhard Avenue, Avenel, New Jersey 07001

© Salamander Books Ltd, 1995

ISBN 0-517-14179-5

A CIP catalog record for this book is available from the
Library of Congress.

All correspondence concerning the content of this
volume should be addressed to Salamander Books Ltd.

CREDITS
Author: Anna Griffiths
Project Manager: Jane Donovan
Editor: Samantha Gray
Design: Watermark
Communications Group Ltd
Photographer: Jon Stewart
Stylist: Barbara Stewart
Photography on pages
24, 25, 37, 90–93 by
Marie-Louise Avery
Illustrations: Steve Dew
& Terry Evans
Originated, printed
and bound in Italy

Contents

Introduction

The most treasured heirlooms are often those with strong memories of the giver attached to them - perhaps a precious silver thimble from an old aunt who was a keen seamstress, or a snowy white damask tablecloth from a rather house-proud grandmother. Such keepsakes are often given with strict instructions on how to keep them in pristine condition! In my own case, I treasure some extremely fine, long paintbrushes that my grandfather gave me when he was no longer able to paint. I remember him using them and wiping them clean on the wall of his workshop - the wall was a work of modern art!

To give something you have made to a member of your family is an act of faith and hope that they will remember you in the years ahead. There are many beautiful projects to make in this book for your family and friends, some using traditional techniques and others which have a more contemporary feel.

I have revived some Victorian skills too - for example, the pincushions stuffed with sawdust and decorated with pins and lace, and the favorite ladylike pastime of decoupage on an appealing hatbox. I also hope that I have pulled at a few heartstrings with a favorite technique of the 1920s - ribbon-weaving - used to make a love-letter purse and a ring pillow for a wedding. There is also an enchanting christening gown and a quilt for a baby, and, for children of all ages, there is a classic teddy bear and a rag doll.

Once you have swallowed the lump in your throat, you will be pleased to know that beach vacations are remembered with projects for budding shell and stamp collectors in the form of delightful small boxes. I have also encouraged thrift with a pretty cottage coin bank and tidiness with a sock bag in the shape of an irresistible duck! The only thing left to do is to curl up with one of the large, comfortable patchwork pillows and enter your best-loved recipes and gardening tips into the made-for-the-purpose books featured on the following pages; your relatives are sure to enjoy reading them in the years to come.

There are many more projects to choose from, and nothing is prohibitively expensive to make. I hope that you will be inspired to try one or two techniques that you have not attempted before. The projects have clear, instructive diagrams to help you through any tricky steps, and there is a useful section of techniques at the back of the book. The invitation to do this book came to me a few months after a major operation. In its preparation, I had to stretch quite a few friendships and coerce my family into helping with some of the designs and projects. Long-distance telephone calls and numerous interrupted mealtimes were the order of the day for quite some time. However, all those involved claimed to have enjoyed making up the projects, and I hope you will too.

Good luck with your projects - I hope that you have as much fun with them as I have had.

Anna Griffiths

Romantic Memories

The enchanting projects featured in this chapter will conjure up
feelings of nostalgia and memories of sweet romance. A glamorous
evening bag will become a memento of special nights out and
love letters can be kept in a frothy, lace-edged pochette, to be brought
out and reread through the years to come. Keepsakes to treasure
from a wedding day include a cream and white ribbon-covered
pillow for presenting the ring and the "something blue" in the
form of a frilly garter. In addition, the wedding photograph album
cover and the sampler provide a suitably elegant record of a day
you will want to remember.

Ring Pillow

This delightful ring pillow will insure that the bride's wedding ring is presented in style, and it is light enough to be carried by even the smallest of bridesmaids! The technique used is ribbon-weaving, a traditional skill that has many exciting possibilities due to the wonderful range of ribbons available today. Your colors may be taken from the bridal gown and, perhaps, coordinated with the flowers and table favors for a really elegant effect.

Finished size: 8¼ x 8¼in (21 x 21cm)

Materials

1½yd (1.40m) of each of the following
Offray ribbons:
Single-face satin, ¼in (7mm) wide,
in ivory (shade 810) and white (shade 29)
Single-face satin, ⅝in (15mm) wide,
in ivory (shade 810) and white (shade 29)

Mediumweight fusible interfacing, 10 x 10in
(25 x 25cm) square
Sharp, fine dressmaker's pins
Small safety pin
Ruffled ivory lace, 1 yd (92cm) in length,
½in (1.2cm) wide
White sewing thread
Sewing needle
Satin, 10 x 10in (25 x 25cm) square,
for the backing
Single-face white satin ribbon, 20in (51cm)
in length, ¼in (7mm) wide, for the bow
Four Offray white ribbon roses
Batting, 9 x 9in (23 x 23cm) square and about
1in (2.5cm) thick

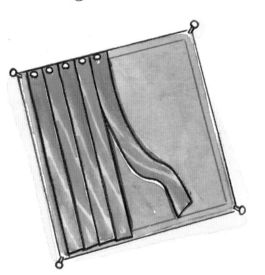

Pin the ribbons onto the top edge of the interfacing and baste across.

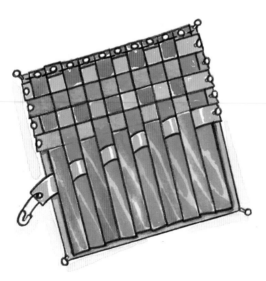

The horizontal ribbons are woven across - over one, under one - with the aid of a safety pin.

To weave the pillow

Cut the ribbons into 10in (25cm) lengths. Lay the interfacing, adhesive side up, on your work surface. Pin the ribbons to the top edge in the following order: wide white, narrow ivory, narrow white, wide ivory, narrow white, narrow ivory. Repeat across the top, keeping each ribbon close to the next (see artwork, top left). Baste to hold in place.

Begin weaving over the rows of ribbons by pinning a small safety pin to one end of the first ribbon and taking it under one ribbon and over the next, all the way across. Pin in place. Continue in this way in a set sequence of colors across the top ribbons, until you have completed the weaving (see artwork, below left).

Set the iron to wool. Cover the weaving with a clean cloth before pressing to bond the ribbons to the interfacing. Do not push the iron around or you will disturb the ribbons (see artwork, page 12). Remove the pins and turn the weaving over. Steam-press the back of the weaving, using a steam iron or a damp cloth and a hot iron.

To make up the pillow

Pin the lace to the edge of the ribbon piece, facing inward and with right sides together. Baste all around. Pin the backing onto the pillow front and stitch on three sides. Clip the corners and turn right sides out. Gently push out the corners to make a neat square, then press, if necessary, with a cool iron on the backing side. Fold the length of ribbon for the bow in half and stitch to the center of the pillow; tie into a bow. Slide the batting into the pillow and turn in the ends to close. Pin and slipstitch (see Techniques, page 103). Sew the roses at each corner.

Love-Letter Pochette

This pretty pochette could hold cherished love letters or family correspondence. It is made from a simple rectangle of ribbon-weaving, stitched up the sides and fastened with ribbons, and decorated with a dainty lace edge. It will lend itself to other uses too, like carrying fine silk scarves and hose on overnight trips, or it could be used to hold writing paper and envelopes.

Finished size: 6½ x 9in (17 x 23cm)

Materials

Offray ribbon in the following sizes and colors:
Single-face satin, 4⅜yd (4m) in length,
⅝in (15mm) wide, in bluebell (shade 307)
Single-face satin, 4⅜yd (4m) in length,
⅝in (15mm) wide, in iris (shade 447)
Single-face satin, 4⅜yd (4m) in length,
⅝in (15mm) wide, in lilac mist (shade 420)
Double-face satin, 1yd (91cm) in length,
⅜in (9mm) wide, in bluebell (shade 307)
Sharp, fine dressmaker's pins
Mediumweight fusible interfacing,
9½ x 13in (24 x 33cm)
Ruffled lace, 46in (116cm) in length,
¾in (2cm) wide
Polyester lining fabric, 9½ x 13in (24 x 33cm)
Sewing thread in color to match lining
Sewing needle

Shiny satin ribbons have been used for the pochette. For a softer look, taffeta or antique ribbons are another option.

To weave the pochette

Cut five lengths of 13in (33cm) from each color of the ⅝in (15mm) wide ribbons. Lay the interfacing, adhesive side up, on your work surface. Pin the ribbons side by side at one narrow end in the following sequence: lilac mist, iris, bluebell. Repeat

Lightly press the face of the weaving through a thin cloth onto the adhesive interfacing, before pressing more firmly on the back.

along the top edge to cover the interfacing. Weave the ribbons across from side to side and in the set color sequence, with the same basic weave pattern used for the Ring Pillow. Follow the Ring Pillow instructions for finishing. You will now have a rectangle of woven ribbon, trimmed and ready for the next stage.

Making up the pochette

Lay the weaving, right side up, on the work surface and begin to pin the lace trim around it, facing inward and overlapping the ends slightly: then baste in position. Cut the narrow ribbon into four pieces, then pin each one 2in (5cm) in from the short side edges of the weaving, facing inward.

Place the lining on top of the lace and woven ribbon, right sides together. Pin in place, making sure that the trim and the seam align. Baste carefully to prevent the ribbons slipping; leave a small opening of 4in (10cm) unstitched. Machine-stitch over the basting, then clip the corners and turn right sides out. Push out the corners gently - a round-ended instrument, such as a pen cap, is good for this purpose - and then press lightly with a cool iron. Fold the weaving in half right side out, pin together, and machine-stitch as close to the edge of the weaving as possible.

Right *The technique of ribbon-weaving is used here to make a lovely pochette for letters, which has a tie fastening on top.*

Blue Evening Bag

An elegant handbag for evening functions is always invaluable, and the sophisticated appearance of this one will suit any special occasion. The ribbon-weaving is diagonal, with a variety of widths and shades of ribbon to add depth and interest.

Finished size: 5½ x 10in (15 x 26.5cm)

Materials

Offray ribbons in the following colors and sizes:
Taffeta, 2¾yd (2.50m) in length, ⅝in (15mm) wide, in royal blue (shade 350)
Double-face satin, 2¾yd (2.50m) in length, ⅞in (23mm) wide, in royal blue (shade 350)
Double-face satin, 2¾yd (2.50m) in length, ¼in (7mm) wide, in light navy (shade 365)
Double-face satin, 2¾yd (2.50m) in length, ⅞in (23mm) wide, in light navy (shade 365)

Mediumweight fusible interfacing, 14 x 10½in (36 x 27cm), in charcoal
Dressmaker's pins
Lining, 14 x 10½in (36 x 27cm), in royal blue
Button, ¾in (2cm)
Sewing thread in color to match lining
Sewing needle

Make a feature of the button fastening by choosing one with some surface interest, as here, or for a really glittery effect, choose faux diamonds or diamanté.

Pin the ribbons in sequence diagonally across the interfacing, working from left to right before weaving the horizontal ribbons across.

Weaving the bag

Lay the interfacing with adhesive side up. Decide on the sequence for the ribbons and lay them out in that order on your work table. Take the first one and pin across the top corners from left to right (see artwork, below left); cut off any additional length, leaving a small allowance. Pin the next one in your sequence below the first one, then continue until you have covered the rectangle.

Weave across in the same way as for the Love-Letter Pochette, finishing as described previously. Pin on a folded piece of narrow ribbon at the center on one narrow side, facing inward, for the button loop. Make sure that the button will go through it first, then pin on the lining and proceed as for the Love-Letter Pochette. Finish by turning in the opening and slipstitching neatly with matching thread to close.

Fold over 5in (12.5cm) to the front and then pin. Using matching thread in a fine sewing needle, stitch the front to the back with small, close stitches, through the lining only if possible. Find the right position for the button and stitch it firmly in place to finish the handbag.

Alternative colors for this evening bag could range from deep, rusty browns and rich chocolate, dark green-shot taffeta with dark gray, to a summer theme of soft honey shades mixed with cream.

Right *Make this elegant, deep blue handbag in matt taffeta with shiny satin ribbons in one evening and use it the next!*

Bridal Garter

"Something old, something new, something borrowed, something blue," goes the saying about what is needed to insure good luck for the bride on her wedding day. A bridal garter trimmed with blue is just what is wanted for the "something blue." It can be made to go over or under the knee, depending on the dress style. Trim it with beads and roses, or make it with lots of frilly lace and bows.

To slim down the fullness of the garter without losing its sumptuous look, simply reduce the length of lace used.

Materials

FOR THE CREAM LACE GARTER

The exact quantities you will need are dependent on the size of the leg measurement. Allow a minimum of 18in (46cm) for the finished size of an over-the-knee garter.
Offray single-face blue satin ribbon (shade 305), 12in (30cm) in length, ⅝in (15mm) wide
Cream soft lace, 28in (71cm) in length, 2½in (6.5cm) wide
Small safety pin
Elastic, 18in (46cm) in length, ½in (1.2cm) wide
Sewing thread in matching color
Sewing needle
Offray single-face blue satin ribbon (shade 305), 12in (30cm) in length, ³⁄₁₆in (5mm) wide
Offray cream ribbon (shade 810), 12in (30cm) in length, ¹⁄₁₆in (1.5mm) wide
Small pearl beads

Choosing lace and ribbons

Ideally the lace and ribbons should be as soft as possible to avoid discomfort. Look out for silk lace and ribbons, and refurbish them by hand-washing in pure soap; or, use scraps of fabric from your own wedding dress or veil to make a garter.

Cut out a small motif from spare lace. Trim it neatly all around. Sew a ribbon rose in the center with short lengths of narrow ribbon behind it. Around the edge, sew on evenly spaced pearl beads. Now sew the motif onto the garter.

To make the cream lace garter

Place the blue ribbon on top of the lace and pin in position; work a zigzag stitch along either side of the ribbon. Overlap the ends of the lace and secure with small neat hand-stitches, leaving the ribbon area unstitched. Attach a safety pin to one end of the elastic and thread it through the ribbon casing, stitching both the ends to secure. Cut the two narrow ribbons in half and make two double bows from each pair. Stitch firmly to the ribbon, after spreading the gathers out equally, then stitch two pearl beads onto each bow center.

Materials

FOR THE WHITE LACE AND ROSES GARTER

White lace with a motif pattern, 19in (48cm) in length, 2in (5cm) wide
Small, sharp scissors
One blue Offray ribbon rosebud
Sewing thread in matching color
Sewing needle
Small pearl beads
Offray single-face blue satin ribbon (shade 7752), 12in (30cm) in length, ¼in (7mm) wide
Offray single-face light-blue satin ribbon (shade 305), 12in (30cm) in length, ¼in (7mm) wide
Elastic, 18in (46cm) in length, ½in (1.2cm) wide
Offray single-face blue satin ribbon, 18in (46cm) in length, ⅝in (15mm) wide
Two white Offray ribbon rosebuds

Right *This light, frothy concoction of a bridal garter has a lace motif with trailing ribbons, pearls, and a rose on the front.*

To make the white lace and roses garter

Cut 1in (2.5cm) from the end of the lace, and cut out one motif with small sharp scissors. Stitch the blue rosebud in the center, with small pearl beads all around the outside. Make a diagonal cut to the narrow ribbons at each end and fold in half; stitch these behind the rosebud (see artwork, page 16).

Lay the wide ribbon down the center of the lace and straight stitch close to the edge either side. Join the lace only with small stitches. Thread the elastic through the ribbon and stitch firmly at both ends; join and stitch the ends. Stitch the rose motif in the center with the white roses either side.

Wedding Sampler

Counted cross-stitch is used for this pretty sampler, with its ribbon edge. It is worked on a fine fabric, which creates good definition in the shapes of the letters and patterns.

Samplers were originally known as "examplars," small embroidered panels, which have been made from the seventeenth century to the present day. Young girls practiced their needlework skills on these small pieces, often featuring the alphabet, a verse, and their name. The sampler here is designed to be stitched to celebrate a wedding, so there is a small box outlined on either side for initials - simply take the pattern of the letter in the alphabet from the chart on the following pages to make the appropriate initial.

Finished size: 13 x 9¾in (33 x 25cm)

Materials
Ivory evenweave linen, 32 threads to the inch, 18 x 18in (46 x 46cm) square
Tapestry needle, no. 24
Basting thread
Masking tape or seam binding
DMC stranded floss in the following quantities and shades:
Two skeins, raspberry (shade 316)
Two skeins, pale raspberry (shade 3727)
One skein, green (shade 3052)
One skein, lilac (shade 3041)
One skein, cream (shade 677)
One skein, corn (shade 676)
One skein, dark green (shade 3053)
One skein, plum (shade 3726)
Embroidery frame
Sewing thread

Outlining with backstitch or Holbein stitch around the cross-stitch embroidery gives it definition: the ribbon border is a good example.

Soft pretty colors on a natural linen fabric enhance this gothic-style lettering.

Preparation
Press the linen flat. Mark the center with vertical and horizontal lines of basting stitches, using a length of sewing thread threaded through a tapestry needle, and working from top to bottom and from side to side. It is vital that these basting lines are accurate because you will count the pattern from them. Bind the edges of the linen with masking tape or seam binding.

Working the embroidery
Use two strands in the needle for the cross-stitch and one strand in the needle for the backstitch.

Look at the chart and at the key: check to see if you have all the colors you need and where they go. Start by stitching the first letter. Count from the center line to find the right position to begin stitching, and count the spaces in between carefully as you work the cross-stitching. Finish each row by working either side of the basted line. Work each row of letters from the chart before going on to the patterns and the ribbon edge.

Check the back of the work for hanging threads, and trim them off to prevent them showing through on the front once the sampler is framed. Press the finished work on the back with a hot iron to remove all creases. Mount the embroidery in a picture frame of your choice.

Right Gentle colors and easy stitches will insure that this sampler appeals to anyone who wants to make a long-lasting and much-appreciated gift.

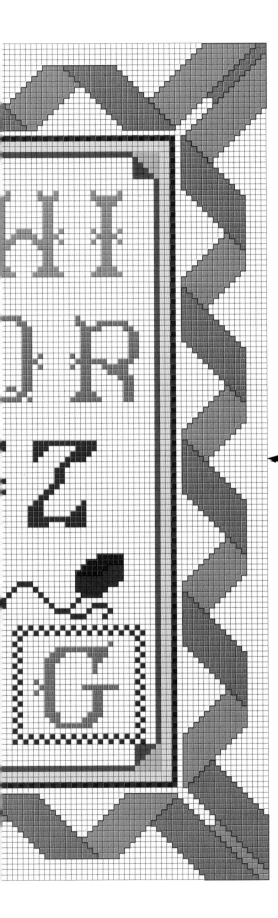

Traditional Samplers

A personalised sampler is one of the most delightful forms of embroidery and certainly one which will survive the ravages of time. Samplers dating back to the 16th century have been discovered, although they were probably stitched with much labor, love and care long before that.

The reason why many antique samplers have kept their pristine condition over the years is because they were first regarded as stitch records or teaching pieces. Often worked by children, they were usually stored away from the light in a drawer, rather than being displayed on a wall for family and friends to enjoy. In the early days when women were often denied an education, the sampler was the sole means of teaching young girls how to read and write.

Personal character is the secret of the great appeal of samplers. Quite often they serve as a mini biography recording the details of the maker's life: a house or a school, favorite flowers, the name and age of the embroiderer, and the village or town in which she lived. Some samplers

have even been known to include severe warnings to sinners!

Whether you make a wedding sampler to celebrate your own marriage or that of a friend or relative, you can be sure that it will become a precious part of family history.

Collecting antique samplers

Once you have created your own sampler, you may well become interested in researching and even collecting heirloom samplers. You need expert advice if you wish to make an investment and hope that your sampler will appreciate in value.

There are many excellent books which cover the history of embroidery, and of samplers in particular. You can learn how to identify different types of materials and threads. Visit museums and famous collections to study the standard of workmanship and wherever possible, look closely at examples of samplers. You may be tempted to purchase a sampler from a private auction or individual. Check the piece carefully and be sure to take into account the age, standard of workmanship and condition of the work before agreeing a price. Remember that the lack of a signature or date on a sampler does not necessarily mean that the sampler is of a lesser value. If you really like a sampler, but it has little or no commercial value, why not buy it because you love it and because it has some rarity?

DMC Stranded Floss

Raspberry 316
Pale Raspberry 3727
Plum 3726
Lilac 3041
Pale Lilac 3042
Cream 677
Corn 676
Dark Green 3053
Green 3052

Wedding Album Cover

Photographs of your - or a member of your family's - wedding will become a unique heirloom when mounted in this beautiful quilted cover. Raw silk is used as the base for the design of two birds and a ring - a simple outline effectively worked in English quilting and finished with a gold bow. You can adjust the basic instructions to fit most sizes of album.

The instructions are given for a 11½ x 12in (29 x 31cm) wedding album

❦

Materials
Photograph album or folder
Ruler
Paper
Pencil
Scissors
Cream silk fabric, 36 x 14½in (91 x 37cm)
White cotton backing fabric,
36 x 14½in (91 x 37cm)
Tracing paper
Felt-tip pen
Hard pencil or quilter's pencil
2 oz (56g) synthetic batting,
36 x 14½in (91 x 37cm)
Dressmaker's pins
Basting thread
One skein cream Coats Anchor
stranded floss (shade 275)
Quilting or stretcher frame (optional)
Offray grosgrain striped gold ribbon (shade c2),
⅝yd (1/2m) in length, ⅝in (15mm) wide

❦

Making the paper pattern
Measure the width of the front, back, and spine of the album, adding 5in (13cm) either end for the inside flap. Measure the

This striped gold grosgrain ribbon makes the album cover look very elegant; other colors particular to your wedding would look equally impressive.

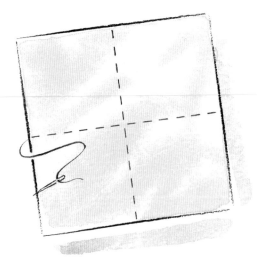

Turn the album cover to the right side and slipstitch the seam allowance at the bottom edge back onto the lining.

height and add 1in (2.5cm) top and bottom for the turnings. Mark the foldlines for the flaps and the position of the spine. Cut a paper pattern from these measurements to cut out the silk and cotton fabrics.

Preparation and quilting
Mark the foldlines and the position of the spine on the cream silk fabric. Trace the design (see template, page 111) in felt-tip pen onto paper, or photocopy it, and place beneath the cream silk fabric, 4½in (12cm) from the top edge and centered between the foldline of the front flap and the spine. Trace the outline onto the fabric using a hard pencil or quilter's pencil. Assemble the silk fabric on top of the batting, which, in turn, is on top of the backing fabric. Smooth the fabrics from the center and pin. Work a 4in (10cm) grid of basting stitches over the surface. Baste around the perimeter.

To quilt, work even backstitches on the marked lines, using two strands of cream stranded floss.

Making up the cover
Neaten both the top and bottom edges, overcasting by hand or machine zigzag. Hem at each end. Fold the flaps, right sides together, along the foldlines, and stitch the corners from the fold edge. Trim away the excess fabric and batting. Fold over the top and bottom hems, and stitch. Turn cover right side out, slipstitch the bottom edge, remove the basting threads, and insert the album (see artwork, left). Make a flat bow to go under the love birds. Pin and stitch it in place, taking the thread through to the back of the cover and leaving the top of the bow free; cut off the ends diagonally to fit the book.

Tea-Dyed Heart Pillow

This lovely heart-shaped pillow was made with butter muslin and lace dyed in tea to give it an aged, old-world appearance. The pillow has pin tucks and lace panels decorating the front, and a deep, gathered lacy edging. Exquisite real pearl buttons are sewn on the front of the pillow.

Where to find lace

You can buy new lace that is made from old patterns in good sewing stores and department stores, but for an authentic nostalgic effect, you may want to source old lace. Look out for odd pieces of lace in antique, thrift or secondhand stores, or go to rummage sales and auctions. The big auction houses hold special textile auctions where you can pick up a case of lace. Old lace hankies and antimacassars can all be turned into pillow covers. Do not reject a piece of lace because it has rust marks, because these can be covered up with another piece of lace. If a piece of lace has been a cuff or collar, it may be slightly gathered, and is therefore best used as a ruffle for a pillow.

The care of lace

Old lace should be kept in a dry, warm atmosphere, and, if it is stored for any

Materials
Heart-shaped pillow form
Butter muslin
Scissors
Tailor's chalk
Sewing thread in matching color
Lace
Dressmaker's pins
Pearl buttons

It is easy to dye lace and butter muslin in strong tea or coffee. You can attain the shade you desire by the length of time you soak the fabric.

Lace can be hung outside immediately after dyeing, but you will then have to rinse it and gently pull it into shape, leaving it flat to dry.

length of time, it should be taken out and aired at frequent intervals to prevent mold forming. Often old lace tends to be a heavy pattern set on a net background. Usually it is the background which wears thin or rips first. In this case, use the non-worn part of the lace as a motif or sew it on to replacement netting.

An old-fashioned method for cleaning lace is to cut a lemon in half and rub it on to any rust marks. If you want to wash lace in a washing machine, put it in a pillowcase and knot the end. This should only be done with fairly robust pieces. Wash delicate lace by pinning it to a linen-covered board, with sufficient pins to keep the lace flat; then dab it gently with a moist sponge. Dissolve detergent flakes in warm water until they form a good lather, then dab the lace again with the detergent until clean. Sponge the detergent off with clean water, and remove as much moisture as possible with a dry sponge.

The lace must not be ironed, but left to dry on the board. Lace can also be pulled gently into shape while still wet and left flat to dry. Very heavy lace may not be sufficiently cleaned by dabbing and may need to be put in a saucepan with a soapy lather, brought to a boil, then rinsed and pinned out to dry.

Dyeing lace

Prepare a very strong pot of tea, allowing the tea to steep for some time. Then pour the tea into a bowl and soak the lace, stirring periodically. The longer you leave the lace, the darker the color will be. For a different color, soak the lace in strong coffee. After the lace has reached a slightly darker shade than you want, remove it and rinse gently. Pin flat on a board to dry.

Making the pillow

You can buy a heart-shaped pillow form in any size you want in most department stores. The amount of muslin fabric and lace you will need depends on the size of the pillow you want, so read the instructions below and be sure to measure your form accurately before you buy fabric. Dye the lace and muslin before cutting the pieces. Cut two heart shapes from butter muslin, slightly larger than the pillow form. If you want to create pin tucks, make the front piece slightly larger than the back. Using tailor's chalk, mark the position for the rows of pin tucks (see Techniques, page 110) on the front piece and sew on the right side of the fabric. Place the front pillow piece on top of the back and check they are now the same size. If not, trim off excess fabric from the larger piece. Cut pieces of lace to decorate the front of the pillow and sew them on by hand. Sew pearl buttons at the apex points of the lace.

To make the ruffle, cut a piece of butter muslin twice the depth you want the finished ruffle to be, plus ⅜in (1cm) seam allowance, and 2½ times the perimeter of the pillow form. This will make a full ruffle. The length of the lace should measure the same length as the fabric frill. Fold the muslin in half lengthwise and place the lace on top of it.

Using a large running stitch, sew through the three thicknesses, along the raw edge of the muslin. Draw up the running stitches and pin the gathers on the right side of the pillow front. Baste the ruffle into position. With right sides together, pin the front and back pillow pieces together. Make sure the ruffle is facing inward, and sew the front to the back around three and a half sides.

Snip into the apex and indentation of the heart, and turn the cover right sides out. Insert the form and close up the opening.

Right: *This delicate heart-shaped pillow suits tea-dyed fabric, but you can make it any shape.*

From Generation to Generation

In this chapter you will find a selection of projects you can make and then keep in the family. For instance, your favorite recipes and gardening tips can be recorded in special, purpose-made books, rather than in a tumbling pile of old notebooks! Keep the elegant, scented hanger sachet and the beautiful pincushions for yourself until there is someone in the family who expresses an interest in them, or you could make extra ones as gifts - the technique is very simple. And why not have fun with the rest of the family making the Christmas ornaments?

Family Recipe Book

It is always fascinating to read recipes from another age; those from the Depression period tell a very different story than those collected during the 1950s. This elegant recipe book is destined to be handed down through several generations, and filled with well-loved family mealtime favorites; it even has a little pocket inside to put in recipes collected from magazines and kept safely until written in.

Materials
*Hardback book,
about 11½ x 8¼in (29 x 21cm)
One sheet of medium-thick paperboard
¹⁄₁₆in (1.5 - 2mm)
Craft knife
Cutting edge and board
Masking tape
Fabric for wrapping the covers,
45 x 16in (115 x 40cm)
Polyvinyl white glue
Scissors
Thick paper*

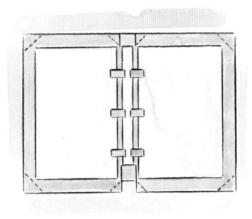

The covers and the spine are kept in position before gluing with strips of masking tape.

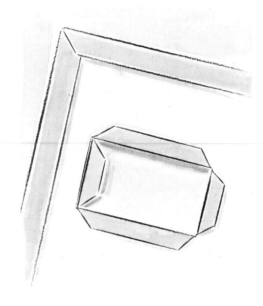

The mitered corners over the window are turned to the inside and glued in place.

To make the book jacket covers
Mark the measurements of the book to be covered, back, front and spine, on the paperboard. With a craft knife, cut out two covers and one spine, taking care to be neat and accurate. Mark out a "window" shape on the front cover, which is slightly smaller than the bookplate, which goes behind it.

Position the two covers and spine on the book and tape them together (see artwork, top), making sure that the gap between them is sufficient for the folding of book - the gap may be as much as ⅜in (6-7mm).

Carefully lay the whole constructed piece onto the fabric and cut around it, leaving a minimum allowance of ¾ - 1¼in (2.5 - 3cm). Peel off the masking tape from the board construction and glue each piece of board onto the fabric.

To make the bookplate window
Carefully cut through the fabric over the window, using a 45° cut into the corners so you can fold over the fabric and glue to the inside. This will create a neat rectangular opening (see artwork, below left).

Assembling the book cover on the book
Cut through the overhanging fabric at the top spine, making just two parallel cuts inward. Fold the fabric over the spine board neatly, and glue. Repeat at the bottom edge. Now glue the two outer covers directly onto the cover itself, using plenty of polyvinyl glue applied evenly.

Glue the flaps in place over the edges of the book cover. Miter the corners where necessary to achieve a tidy result.

The inside endpapers and pocket
Measure the inside front page of the book, and double the measurement. Mark this size out on thick paper, which should be in a shade which goes well with the outer fabric cover. Cut out two double pages.

To make a triangular pocket, cut out a piece of the same thickness of paper, two-thirds of the height of the book so that it makes a square, adding about ⅝in (20mm) margin. Fold the paper diagonally and firmly crease. Glue it in position over the front endpaper. Apply glue to the front endpaper and press down firmly; repeat with the back endpaper. Leave evenly weighted down for a day.

Garden
Record Book

This elegant book could contain a record of the family gardening habits of one generation or more. The pressed flower design on the front will be a permanent record of the garden you picked the flowers from, with delphiniums, little roses, and ivy displayed in an elegant arc. Inside, note down all the things that fascinate gardeners of every generation: what was planted where, and when, with planting tips and suggestions. Stick in seed packets and make small drawings to create a unique and enchanting diary of a garden.

❧

Materials

Selection of flowers, buds and leaves
Flower press (optional)
Sheets of blotting paper (absorbent paper)
Old telephone books, or other large, heavy books
A sheet of thin paperboard, the size of the book front you are going to cover
Two or three fine-haired paintbrushes
(children's paintbrushes are fine)
Tweezers
Rubber-based glue
Wooden toothpicks
Small, sharp pointed scissors or craft knife
Sheet of protective, adhesive film with a "peel-off" backing
One hardback notebook,
11½ x 8¼in (29 x 21cm)
Polyvinyl white glue and glue brush
One sheet of Florentine marbled paper
Scissors or a craft knife
Cutting edge and board
Gold felt-tip pen (optional)

❧

When to pick

The best time to pick flowers is at noon when the morning dew has dried away. Sunny days are ideal. Rainy days are to be avoided - allow a full dry day afterward before picking. If you must pick on a damp day, snip off the whole stems and stand in water until the flowers have dried off; even then, when you come to press them, you may have to change them from one sheet of blotting paper to another to take away the excess moisture. Pick other

Above *Here a selection of pressed flowers is ready for use.*

Right *Memories of gardens past are stored in this beautiful book.*

parts of plants as well as the flowers, such as buds, leaves, trailing stems, and grasses, to give a variety of shapes.

When you pick in woodlands, first make sure that you check the official list of protected and endangered species for the area you want to pick in. If you are picking in your own garden, lay the flowers and leaves in a basket and press them as soon after cutting as you can. Florists' flowers and leaves are another source of material, and florists will often give you the cuttings left over from arrangements, which may have a lot of pieces that you can use. The flowers pressed for the book here are delphiniums, single-petaled roses, larkspur, rose of Sharon, (*Hypericum calycinum*) ivy, and clematis stems and buds.

How to press

Separate some flower heads from their stalks to reduce the bulk, or because they are more useful as heads only. Press other flowers with stalks intact, keeping the natural shape and curves. Large-headed flowers with thick centers can have their petals taken off separately, and, when re-assembled, a false middle made from another small flower can be used. Place the flowers, leaves, and so on in between two sheets of blotting paper, and then in between the pages of a heavy book.

Make marker tags for the types of flowers to help you when you come to make up the design. When the book is comfortably full, not bursting, weigh it down with bricks, or another heavy object, and leave it in a dry place for about four to six weeks. The same time lapse should occur if you use a flower press.

The design

Take out the sheets of flowers and leaves that you want in your design, and decide what the best shape should be for the book front. Mark out the area of the design on thin board, then begin to arrange the dried material onto it with either the tweezers or a paintbrush. Move pieces around carefully, noting the natural curves and bends of the stems and tendrils, until the whole design is as you want it. If you can not glue the pieces down immediately, cover with a sheet of blotting paper until you are ready. Begin to stick down your

design by lifting each piece with either a paintbrush or tweezers and putting a small dot of glue on the back with a toothpick. Press each piece into position.

Cut out a piece of protective film the same size as the board. Next unpeel the top edge and press onto the top of the board. Gradually peel downward, and press and smooth down at the same time. Smooth out any bubbles on the surface, making sure that the film covers every part of the design. The film protects the dried flower arrangement, both from damage and discoloring, and is easy to wipe clean.

After the window is cut, the bookplate, which is larger than the opening, can be positioned carefully before gluing.

To make the garden record book

Trim the pressed flower board to a size ¼in (5mm) smaller in width and height to the book cover. Open the book and lay it on the covering paper. Mark out a corresponding shape that is 1in (2.5cm) larger all around than the book itself. Cut this out with scissors or a craft knife. To assess the depth of the mitered corners of the book cover, place the open book again onto the covering paper and mark out the 45° miters on the corners. It is important not to cut these corners too deep – allow ³⁄₁₆in (3mm), otherwise the book's corners will be exposed. Mark the thickness of the spine on the inside of the paper, so that an allowance for a turning at top and bottom edges can be made.

On the front face of the cover, mark out the "window" shape, which will go over the flower design. This can be any shape you like, but it should be decided before the flower arrangement is made.

Cut out the "window" carefully with the craft knife. At this point, a gold line can be drawn around the "window" with a felt-tip pen, if you want.

Cut two rectangles for the inside covers; these are ½in (1cm) shorter in both width and height than the book. Glue the back of the pressed flower board and position on the front of the book. Press and hold down around the design until it is firmly stuck.

Lay the cover on a clean work surface. Apply glue to the inside front face and place the opened book onto it, making sure that it is square and central to the corners. Press and turn the corners over to the inside. Repeat with the back and the spine - the latter will need to be cut and trimmed to make it fit at the top. Apply the two endpapers by gluing and pressing down firmly as before.

Victorian Pincushion

These lovely pincushions make elegant accessories to hold hat pins on your dressing table, or keep one with your sewing kit for dressmaker's pins. Choose between the pretty Rose-Cluster Pincushion and the enchanting Lace-Covered Pincushion - each is sure to be treasured through the years to come and would also make an enduring and delightful present.

Materials

FOR BOTH PINCUSHIONS:
½yd (0.5m) cotton velveteen
½yd (0.5m) strong lining
½ pound (225g) fine sawdust,
available from pet stores
Buttonhole or waxed thread

FOR THE LACE-COVERED PINCUSHION:
Dressmaker's pins
Cotton lace, 1¼in (3cm) wide,
14in (36cm) in length
Ruffled lace, 1¼in (3cm) wide,
14in (36cm) in length
Taffeta ribbon, ½in (1.2cm) wide,
14in (36cm) in length
Small beads and sequins
Narrow ribbon

To make the pincushion base

From the velveteen, cut out two circles, about 6in (15cm) in diameter. Cut a side band on the bias, 1¾ x 20in (4 x 50cm). Cut out the circles and band again from the lining. Baste one round piece of lining onto the band of lining fabric, right sides together, and sew around the edge. There will be some overlap at the end. With right sides together, attach the second round

Using a spoon, pour the sawdust carefully into the inner lining of the pincushion until it is very full. Settle the contents by tapping the pincushion gently on a table. Fill again if necessary. Close the opening with small stitches of doubled thread.

Pin the ruffled lace to form a skirt around the side of the pincushion, then pin on the ribbon band. Make sure that all the joins are in exactly the same place. Cover the joins with a bow, which can be single or double, and secure it firmly in place with a ball-headed pin.

piece of lining onto the other side of the band, sewing three-quarters of the way around. Repeat for the velveteen fabric.

Turning both the lining and the velveteen right sides out, place the lining inside the velveteen so that the openings are in the same place. Spoon the sawdust into the inner lining until it is very full. Tap the pincushion gently on a table to settle the contents. Refill, if necessary. Pin the opening together and oversew, using small, tight stitches and doubled thread.

To decorate the Lace-Covered Pincushion

Pin the flat lace to partly cover the top seam, and cover the bottom edge of the flat lace with the ruffled lace so it forms a skirt that just touches the table surface. Make sure that all the joins are in the same place, and cover them with a single or double bow, attached with a ball-headed pin.

The flat lace can be maneuvered into extensions and points once the whole pincushion is pinned; pull out the lace gently so you do not risk tearing it. Make sure that you do not press in pins on top of one another. You should only need about six pins to hold it all in place at the start, and these can be moved about or added to as necessary. Make these adjustments once you have put all the lace and ribbons on, then the pins can be safely removed and repositioned. Place the ruffled lace over the flat lace to cover the bottom edge. Add the ribbon band to finish, with the ribbon bows covering the join.

Right Pincushions have been treasured keepsakes for centuries, passed down through generations from mother to daughter. They can be personalized in many ways, as shown here.

Rose-Cluster Pincushion

Materials
FOR THE ROSE-CLUSTER PINCUSHION,
YOU WILL ALSO NEED:
*Fabric remnants in various colours
and thicknesses
Narrow pieces of chiffon
Matching thread, needle
Indelible gold felt-tip pen*

To make the Rose-Cluster Pincushion

Using the fabric remnants to make the roses, cut strips of fabric about four times as long as they are deep. The size that you want each finished rose to be will determine the size and depth of the strips, so some experimentation is necessary.

With right sides together, fold the fabric in half and sew along one short width. Turn right sides out. Then, keeping the strip folded in half, roll the fabric from the stitched end to form the center of the bud, securing with a few stitches. Gather the fabric at the base, turning and catching it with stitches to fasten. Tuck under the raw end and stitch down.

With tiny stitches, sew the rosebuds onto the green band so they cover the surface completely. Cut a narrow piece of chiffon to sew over the join of the band and the top of the pincushion. To complete the decoration on the top, make dots and squiggles with the gold felt-tip pen; you may also like to write a special message with the date or year if the pincushion is to be a special present commemorating a birthday, or perhaps an important wedding anniversary.

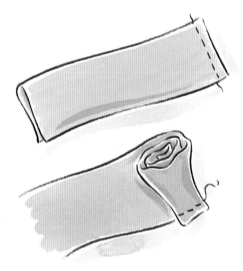

Stitch one end, then turn to the right side and roll from the stitched end to form a bud; secure with a few stitches.

Gather the whole bud at the base and stitch tightly; fold down the raw end and stitch in place.

Roses are as popular as ever, and their appeal as an emblem of love is undoubted, but did you know that they can convey other messages? Red roses mean love but yellow roses mean jealousy, and yellow and pink roses spell out a message of jealousy, perplexity, and grief to the recipient!

For a fragrant pincushion

Why not add some rose essential oil to the sawdust when stuffing the pincushion; then a gentle waft of roses will fill the air every time you push in a pin. This is much simpler than making an old-fashioned recipe like the one I have found from the nineteenth century, which included dried rose petals and lavender, coriander seeds, orris root, cloves, cinnamon sticks, and one pound of oak shavings. All the ingredients were ground to a coarse powder - your blender would never be the same again!

Right *This lovely Rose-Cluster Pincushion is ideal for displaying a collection of antique hat pins.*

Perfumed
Hanger Sachet

*F*ill this pretty embroidered sachet with fragrant dried lavender or other herbs to give a sweet smell to your clothes. The embroidery on the sachet is known as Hardanger and originates in Norway. Its distinctive open-block design is based on geometric shapes, using the fabric to count the pattern. This small beginner's piece will wet your appetite for Hardanger work, and you may want to progress to larger projects. Traditionally, Hardanger embroidery was used to decorate bridal garments and bed linen, but today this lovely hardwearing form of needlework is mostly used on table linen, where the patterns of the embroidery can be seen and admired at their best.

Materials
Two 5in (12.5cm) squares of cream Hardanger fabric, with 24 threads per 1in (2.5 cm)
Cream cotton sewing thread
Very fine-pointed, sharp embroidery scissors
One skein of DMC Coton Perlé No 5, in ecru
Tapestry needle, size 20
Two 5in (12.5cm) squares of fine cotton fabric, preferably in a pastel shade
Small amount of dried lavender, or your chosen herb

The Hardanger technique
Hardanger is a pretty form of openwork embroidery, traditionally worked white on white. Ours is cream, but you can use whatever color scheme you like for an effective result. Designs are based on geometric shapes using the threads of the fabric to count the pattern. Work is always

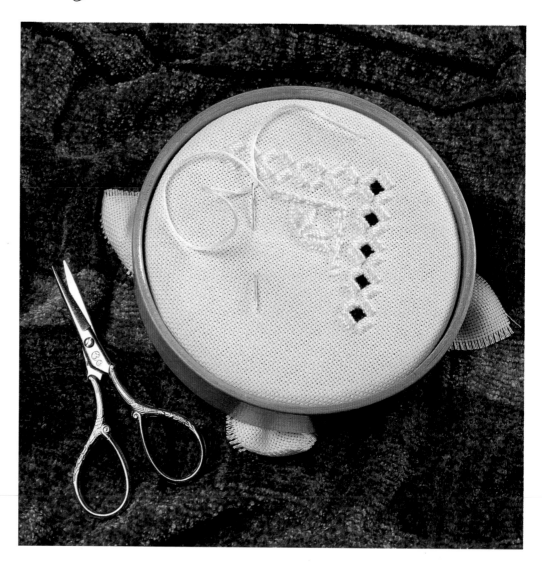

started by outlining the main design with blocks of satin stitch called Kloster blocks. The square area within each motif is cut away and the threads withdrawn. Quite often the open squares are decorated with filling stitches, with surface stitchery between motifs.

Hardanger fabric has a well-defined warp and weft, so to avoid distortion when working, you should use an embroidery

frame; for smaller pieces, an embroidery hoop can be used.

Right *The cutwork holes in Hardanger pieces make the technique ideal for potpourri or lavender sachets; they let the fragrance seep through to perfume the air.*

To work the embroidery

Measure and mark the centers of one square of Hardanger fabric. Either machine zigzag or overcast the raw edges by hand to prevent fraying (see artwork, right). Follow the chart for the accurate position of the stitches in the design, and refer to the key for stitches used. Count from the marked center line to find the starting point for the Kloster blocks. Work all the blocks and the small cross-stitches, then the satin stitch star in the middle. Snip the fabric threads close to the blocks, as shown in the artwork below right. Gently ease the cut threads out from the edges to form the square holes to complete the embroidery.

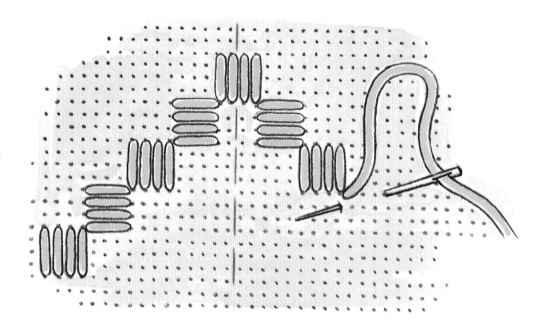

Above, right Count from the center line and work the Kloster blocks, as shown on the chart.

Right Cutting away the centers of the Kloster blocks is nerve-racking at first, but is easier than it looks, provided that you have sharp embroidery scissors. Snip the threads of the fabric close to the blocks and gently ease out the cut threads to form square holes.

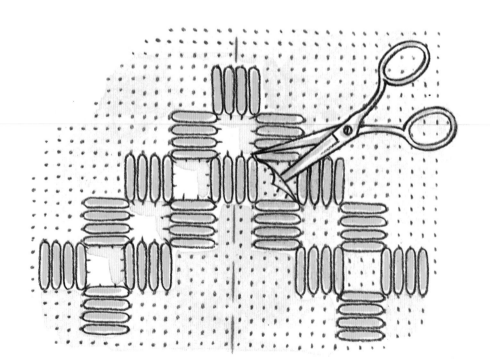

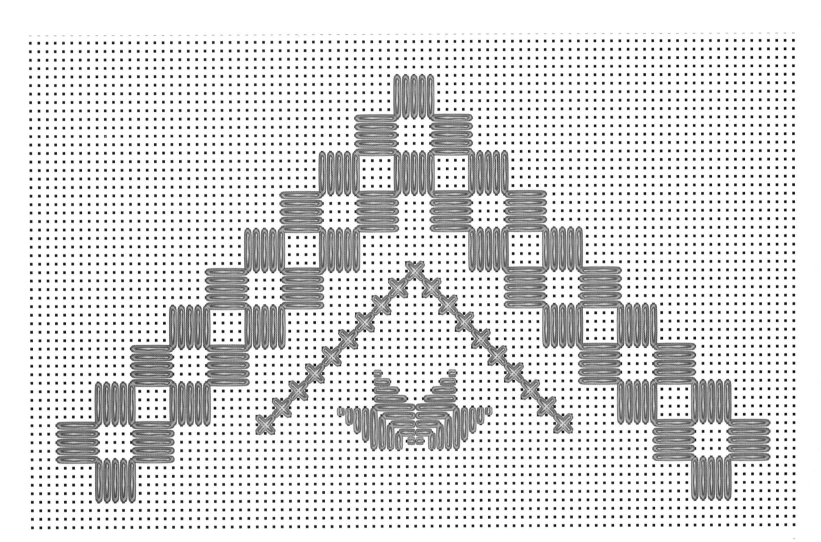

To make up the sachet
The lining.
Place the two lining squares of fabric right sides together, and stitch around three sides with a ½in (1.2cm) seam allowance. Turn right sides out and fill with dried lavender or the herbs of your choice; take care not to overfill or the finished sachet will look lumpy and overstretched. Turn in the seam allowance along the open edge, pin, and stitch to close neatly.

The hanging loop
Knot two 36in (40cm) lengths of coton perlé together at both ends and make into a twisted cord (see Techniques, page 106).

The tassel
Make a tassel with 6in (22 x 15cm) lengths of coton perlé (see Techniques, page 106).

The sachet
Pin the twisted loop at the top of the backing square, so that it straddles both sides of the point. Stitch in place by hand, then position the tassel at the opposite bottom point and stitch in place. Fold both the tassel and the cord into the center of the backing, and place the embroidered front, face down, over the backing. Pin and stitch on three sides, with a seam allowance of ½in (1.2m). Clip the corners and turn to the right side. Place the perfumed bag inside the cover and turn in the seam allowance, then slipstitch using tiny stitches to close.

Special-Occasion
Tablecloth & Napkins

Adorned with bows, this tablecloth and set of napkins give the perfect finishing touch to a table setting. You can make the bows for any size of tablecloth or napkin, to suit a grand occasion or, perhaps, an intimate celebratory meal. For the bow fabric, you could choose one with shiny spots or stripes, or use any exotic scraps you have kept, because you only need a small amount. The bows have added impact with stem stitching in gold thread worked along the edges. Alternatively, you could use silver thread or any other effective color.

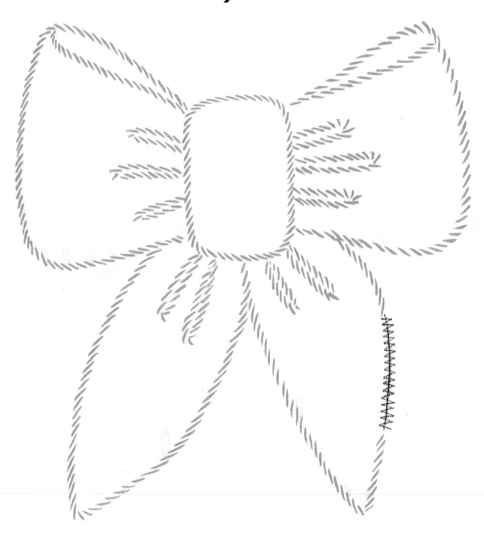

Ideas for the bows

You do not have to position the bows in each corner - for example, three or four bows facing into the center could look elegant on a large tablecloth. Each one could be in a different shade of the same fabric, perhaps the faintest pastel colors of lawn or voile. These could be echoed by small bows on the napkins.

Bows in silver organza at each corner with a setting of silver tableware, would create a beautiful, romantic table display, or you might want to try a gold theme. For a Christmas party, add green plaid bows to a red cloth.

Materials

A tablecloth
Fabric for each bow,
approx. 6 x 6in (15 x 15cm) square
Square of fusible web,
6 x 6in (15 x 15cm) for each bow
Dressmaker's pins
Matching sewing thread
Embroidery thread, Kreinik 002C, in gold

To appliqué the bows

Place the fusible web over the bow template and trace the outline. Repeat until you have the required number of bows. Mark the position for each bow on the tablecloth with a pin. Cut out the bows from the fusible web and iron them onto your chosen bow fabric. Cut out the bows, remove the backing, and pin in position. Bond them to the tablecloth with a medium-hot iron. Press the bows without moving the iron around on the fabric, because this will wrinkle the fusible web.

Stitch all around the main outline of the bow, using matching thread and a close zigzag machine stitch. With a single strand of gold thread, work a close stem stitch outline, including the crease lines inside the bow.

The small bows on the table napkins are worked in the same way as the large ones. Reduce the template on a photocopier.

Collage
Memory Album

Vacations, special events, family recipes, and theater outings are all special moments to treasure, and deserve to be recorded in a unique album. You may like to create a baby book, in which case use pretty printed fabric and baby pictures for the cover. You could use tiny shells on the cover for a beach vacation album or theater and opera tickets for an album to hold old programs. If you choose an album in a different size from the one we have used, simply adjust the amount of a fabric accordingly and follow the same process as below, adapting the measurements to your requirements.

Materials
An inexpensive photo album or scrapbook,
13¾ x 11¾in (35 x 30cm)
Fabric, such as velvet,
satin or cotton, ½yd (0.5m)
Fusible interfacing, ½yd (0.5m)
Basting thread
Sewing needle
Scraps of different patterned fabrics
Lace remnants
Fabric glue
Matching sewing thread
Thin gold wire
Tiny beads or shells (optional)
Ribbon, ½yd (0.5 m) of 4in (10cm) wide

Cut your chosen fabric and interfacing to 35 x 16in (88 x 40cm). Place the interfacing, shiny-side down, on the wrong side of the fabric. Cover with a clean cloth and iron on a cotton setting - this will give the fabric some body. Baste a vertical line

Create your own collage from a collection of family photographs and precious pieces of lace trimmings collected over the years.

Sepia photographs and old lace are sewn onto the front cover in a collage, then gold wire is twisted around the photos and sewn on.

down the center of the interfaced fabric and baste a parallel line 2in (5cm) to the right. This line marks the front edge of the cover.

Use aged fabrics, bits of old lace, organdy, and sepia photographs on the cover, and sew into position or stick on with fabric glue. Twist some gold wire and arrange it in a pattern over your collage, sewing down with tiny stitches. You may also like to sew on tiny beads or shells.

Cut a 12½in (31cm) piece of the 4in (10cm) wide ribbon and baste it down over the vertical, left-hand row of basting stitches, so it stops slightly short of the top and botton of the album. Sew into place with a close zigzag machine stitch. About ½in (1cm) from the ribbon spine, cut down 1⅝in (4.5cm). To make the flaps, fold in the right and left edges by 2¼in (8cm) so the right sides of the fabric are together. Pin and machine-stitch across the fold, 1½in (4cm) below the top edge and above the bottom edge. Trim the folded 2¼in (8cm) of fabric to within ¼in (6mm) of the stitching, turn out to form the sleeves, and push the cover into its jacket.

To finish, glue the center flaps to the inside of the spine and glue the other edges to the inside of the front and back covers. Mark the other three edges of the cover to produce a frame in which to add your appliqué shapes.

Right *A collage album is a perfect way to personalize a family album, and makes the album a thoughtful gift to hand down to younger members of your family. You may like to write a title on the album cover, and you can do so by using a permanent pen on a piece of ribbon and sewing the ribbon onto the cover.*

Traditional Bears

These two traditional-style bears are made from the same pattern, only the type of fur chosen makes them look different. The jointed legs and arms move, and, more unusually, the head can turn from side to side, which gives them character and makes them wonderful for a small child to play with. Both bears are extremely loveable and exactly the right size for a small person to get very attached to!

Furs and fabrics

The fur fabrics used for bear-making are made from man-made fibers, such as acrylic, nylon, and modacrylic. Many of the fabrics have a knitted backing, for easy shaping when stuffing. Always check whether the fabric is washable or must be professionally dry-cleaned.

Materials

FOR A 8IN (20CM) BEAR:
Thin sheet of paper and pen
Craft fur, 10 x 20in (25 x 51cm)
Small, sharp scissors
Dressmaker's pins
Small pieces of felt or velvet for the paws
Embroidery floss or yarn, for the nose and claws
*Two ⅜in (9mm) safety eyes
(or two ¼in (7mm) safety eyes
for a different look)*
*Four ⅞in (20mm) joints and
one 1in (25mm) joint*
*Child-safe polyester stuffing
(about 2oz (50g), depending on type)*

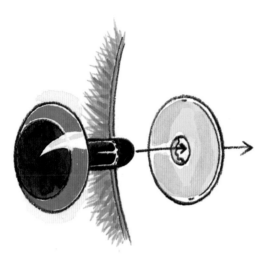

The safety eye is pushed through the fabric and the washer is pushed on firmly from the back.

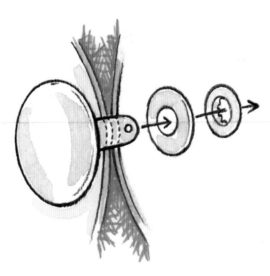

The joint is pushed through from the inside of the arm or leg to the inside of the body. The flat washer is put on, and then the ridged washer is pushed on to fit tightly.

Making the bear

Use a piece of thin paper to copy the trace patterns, and draw with a heavy line. Mark the instructions on each one. Turn the tracing over, and then place another piece of paper on top. Trace the parts that need reversing, and mark these with the instructions as before.

Lay out the pattern pieces on the reverse side of the craft fur, following the layout guide and making sure that the arrows follow the downward grain of the fabric. Pin the pattern pieces to a single layer of fabric, and then cut them out carefully using small, sharp scissors. Mark the positions of the joints and eyes before you take off the pattern pieces.

Head

Join head pieces from A-C, insert the gusset, and join both side heads from B-C, rounding or squaring them off the nose as preferred. Baste pieces together before sewing to prevent the craft fur moving. Leave the neck edge open; turn out. Join the ears in pairs and turn out.

Eyes

Insert the safety eyes into the head, making sure that the washer is pushed tightly against the back of the head so the eye can not be moved. Stuff the head well. Use a strong doubled thread to draw the neck edge closed, and knot firmly.

Right *These small, appealing bears are made from the same pattern, but they each have different fur and the expression on both their faces varies to make them unique.*

Ears

Experiment with the ears in various positions before you sew them on because the character of the bear will alter slightly with each angle. Ladder stitch the ears to the head, turning in the raw edges as you sew (see Techniques, page 100). Use yarn or embroidery floss to embroider your bear's nose. If you have used a long-pile fur, carefully trim away the fur from the muzzle first. Using small scissors, take off a little fur at a time until you reach the base fabric. Use a close stem stitch for the mouth, and a long, close satin stitch for the nose (see Techniques, page 100).

Arms and legs

Attach arm paw pads to the short ends of the arms. Join the arm pieces all around, leaving the shoulder section open for stuffing; turn out. Join the body pieces, leaving the back section open for stuffing; turn out. Now join the leg pieces, leaving the top ends open for stuffing and foot ends open for inserting paw pads. Baste paw pads in place before sewing, easing to fit, then turn out the completed leg.

Joints

Carefully pierce holes for the joints using a sharp awl. Attach arms and legs to the main body section using safety joints and washers. Push the shanked joint from the inside of the arm or leg through to the inside of the body. Place the flat washer over the shank, then push on the ridged washer so it fits tightly. Check that the arms and legs are all facing forward in the correct positions before putting on the final washer. Stuff the arms and legs firmly with child-safe polyester stuffing, and sew

up the openings using ladder stitch for an invisible join.

Finishing

Insert the head joint through the neck circle onto the body, securing with the flat and ridged washers. Stuff the main body firmly, then stitch the back seam using ladder stitch. Stitch the head firmly to the neck circle using ladder stitch; complete a double row of stitching for extra security.

Tease out any fur trapped in the seams with a big needle or a teasel brush to give a seamless appearance. Try not to scratch the eyes as you do this. Embroider the claws if you wish, and finish with a ribbon tied in a bow at the neck of the bear.

Care of your heirloom bear

A much-loved teddy bear is undoubtedly going to get grubby, especially if he has a young owner and is played with a great deal. If both stuffing and fur are washable, and the eyes are plastic safety eyes, the bear can almost certainly be machine-washed at a low-medium temperature. It is advisable to place the toy in a pillowcase first of all, and tie the top tightly. Once washed, the bear will usually be suitable for tumble-drying, but again take the precaution of tying it in a pillowcase and set the machine for delicates.

It is inadvisable to wash bears with growler or squeaker mechanisms inside, or old bears, which may have wood-chip or straw filling, or cardboard joints. Indeed, some antique bears are extremely valuable. The best way to handle older bears is to wash the fur by hand, with mild detergent suds and a sponge or soft brush. Lay the bear on a large towel, dip the sponge in the

soapy suds, and then work in a circular motion, without soaking the bear. Remove the suds with a damp cloth, and dry the bear with a hair-dryer. Comb the fur while it is drying with a fine comb, but be sure to work the fur very gently or you may damage the pile of your bear.

The True Origins of the Teddy Bear

Our fascination with bears probably dates back to the Middle Ages when wild bears were captured and paraded through the streets, and appeared in traveling fairs and circuses. Imagine the fear they would invoke and also the pity for the torture that they endured. By the end of the nineteenth century, they were brought to zoos for the amusement of visitors.

One of the visitors to the zoo at Stuttgart in Germany was a young toy designer called Richard Steiff; he drew the bears and especially the cubs. In 1902, a prototype bear was made with disk joints to move its arms and legs. We wouldn't find this bear very appealing today, because he looked very much like a real bear and we are used to cute and cuddly toy bears. You can easily identify most Steiff bears by a little button at the top of one of the ears.

The 26th President of the United States, Theodore (Teddy) Roosevelt, was a famous bear hunter and is reputed to have been the influence for the first toy bears, created by Morris and Rose Michtom who were novelty and stationery storekeepers. Their designs were distributed all over the United States.

Teddy bear collecting is a serious business, with prices increasing at auctions every year. I love to see well-worn teddies - it is a sign that they have been well-loved. Even if your favorite teddy would be unacceptable at an auction, he will probably be worth a lot to you!

Christmas Ornaments

Light as air, these delicate and brightly colored tree decorations will add a special charm to your seasonal display. They are easy to store and will not damage too readily, so they can be used year after year, becoming a traditional feature of your Christmas tree. They are based on Mexican "God's Eyes" - a folk art technique of wrapping sticks with silk or yarns. Each one has a dark "eye" in the center, hence the name. It was believed that having one of these ornaments in your home would insure that you had boy children! Long toothpicks form the basic structure of the ornaments, with a selection of different threads, including a few glittery ones, wound around them to form the design. The technique is simple and they can be made quickly, so it is an ideal craft to share with children. The secret of success is in the way you put the colors together to make an effective display.

Materials
Polyvinyl white glue
Long wooden toothpicks or short skewers
A selection of threads: stranded embroidery floss, metallic thread, fine knitting yarn, etc.
Sharp scissors

Making the ornaments
Apply a little glue to the center of two toothpicks, form them into a cross, and hold them together until they bond. Now take the dark thread for the eye and, holding it down with one finger, wrap it

To wind the pattern, hold the thread firmly with two fingers of one hand and take it over the first toothpick and under in a half hitch; take it on to the next toothpick and repeat.

To change the color of your thread, place a small drop of glue on the back of the "God's Eye," and press the end down. Attach the next thread to the same point.

twice over one side and then the other to secure. Begin to wind in the pattern by holding the cross firmly with two fingers of one hand and, with the other hand, take the yarn over the first toothpick then under in a half hitch. Take it on to the next toothpick and repeat. Go around and around in this fashion until you have enough to make the "eye."

Change the color by holding the old thread down on the back and applying a minute blob of glue with another toothpick used solely for this purpose. When the glue is tacky, start the new thread at this point so it sticks to the glue as well; if not, just add another small dab. Continue winding and changing color, until the toothpicks are full to the point where they begin to taper. Fasten the last thread with a dab of glue. Complete the ornament by making a hanging loop from one of the threads and gluing it to the back.

Option
These "God's Eyes" can be made on larger wooden skewers or twigs if you find the scale of the ones here too small - just use correspondingly longer threads and yarns.

To finish the ends of larger sticks, why not add yarn tassels (see Techniques, page 105), pom-poms, or trailing curly ribbons? A touch of glitter looks festive, as does fine silver or gold tinsel wound in with the yarn to finish the tassels.

Right *A Christmas tree decorated with "God's Eye" looks gloriously festive.*

Friendship Keepsakes

Gifts for friends are often things that you would like to receive
yourself. Certainly the projects in this chapter will be difficult
to part with, even when they are being given to a much-loved
friend. For example, the gorgeous shell-covered box,
highlighted in gold, would look lovely on any dressing
table, and those special-occasion hats will be very safe
in the delightful rose decoupage box. There are more new
techniques to try out in this chapter, too - from gilding
to needlepoint, quilting and patchwork. So, think of a
deserving friend, and get started!

Gilded Mirror

A gilded frame adds a touch of luxury and opulence to a room, and looks quite different to a frame simply sprayed gold. The traditional method of gilding uses gold leaf; although beautiful, this is both expensive and very difficult to do well. The gilded frame here is created using a technique similar to the traditional one, but much simpler to execute.

Traditional gilding is always done over a layer of pigment called the bole. This is most often black or a red oxide color. Gilding size is applied over the bole and, when the size is tacky, followed by thin sheets of gold leaf which are rubbed down with a gilder's tip and finally burnished. An alternative method is to press metallic powders onto the tacky gold size with a velvet pad, brush away the surplus when dry, and, finally, varnish with clear polish.

For this frame, gilding creams are used, and these are available from art suppliers.

Materials

Lengths of molding, or a ready-made frame
Strong contact glue
Red oxide spray paint (available from hardware stores)
Gilding cream - pale gold, red gold, and copper
Cotton swab (optional)
Mineral spirit and brush (optional)

To gild the frame

Cut lengths of molding to your required size, miter the corners, and glue together. Alternatively, use a ready-made frame. Now spray the frame with red oxide paint and allow to dry thoroughly. Apply the

A wide selection of gilding creams are available, and can be used to create a wealth of different effects – from grand gold pieces to elegant silver or pewter ones.

A collection of frames demonstrates the rich variety of finishes that can be achieved with gilding creams.

gilding cream evenly - a fingertip is best for the purpose - and you will find that a little goes a long way. The effect of the gilding is richer if you combine several colors of gilding cream - here, pale gold is combined with rich red gold, with a little copper applied on top. As the creams are soft, it is easy to combine them.

If the moldings of the frame are very intricate, it may be necessary to use a cotton swab to work cream into tiny crevices; alternatively, thin the cream with a little mineral spirit and use a brush to work it into the crevices.

If you want to give your frame a worn and aged appearance, remove some of the gilding using a cloth moistened with mineral spirit in order to allow some of the red to show through. Allow the frame to dry overnight, then buff with a soft cloth. A little cream may come off on the cloth, but this will not affect the finish - gilding applied in this way is permanent and will not fade or lose its luster.

Options

Gilding creams are available in a wide range of colors, including a series of golds, from pale, greenish gold to rich, reddish gold, and also silver, pewter, copper, and a range of jewel colors, such as amethyst, sapphire, rose quartz, and so on. A great variety of effects can be achieved by combining these colors or using different colors to emphasize particular details. A further possibility for a different look is to use a different colored spray for the underpainting.

Right *A beautiful mirror frame adds elegance to a room. You will be surprised at what you can achieve with gilding techniques.*

Shell-Covered Box

Give this shell-covered box to a friend as a long-lasting reminder of happy times at the seashore, when you shared lazy days collecting shells on the beach and probably found sand in your pockets for years afterward! The soft, lime-washed look with the gilded shells makes it particularly suitable for a dressing table where it could be a useful container for keys, cufflinks, or small pieces of jewelry.

Materials

Shells of all types: flat shells and larger ones in a suitable size for the box
Oval or round lightweight wooden box
Polyvinyl white glue and brush
Small amount of self-hardening clay
Glue gun and glue sticks
White spray paint
A little turpentine
Soft, clean rags
Pearl beads in different sizes
Gold paint - small can of model paint, or a gold felt-tip pen
Small piece of gold ribbon

Covering the box with shells

Sort out the shells, but don't discard the ones with holes in or small pieces broken off, as these can be just as attractive. Put the big ones, such as periwinkle or conch, in the middle of the box lid for height. Arrange the smaller ones around the central group, graduating their size as you move outward. You can try out several options before deciding on the final arrangement, then put all the unwanted shells to one side and cover the work surface with newspaper.

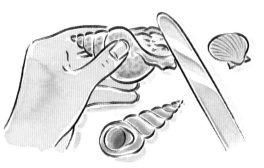

Each shell is painted inside with polyvinyl glue before its back is filled with self-hardening modeling clay, which is scraped level with a knife. This makes a better surface for attaching the shells onto the box. Leave to set before gluing onto the wooden box.

The hanging tab pull prevents any shells becoming dislodged when the box is opened.

Take each chosen shell and paint the inside with polyvinyl glue before filling the backs with self-hardening clay, scraping a knife over the surface to level it off. This will give the shells a flat base so they can be firmly glued onto the box lid. Leave to dry for at least 10-12 hours. Reassemble the shells on the box lid to remind you of their positions. Heat up the glue gun and put a small blob of glue on the back of each shell before sticking it down.

Painting the box

Spray a small part of the box base with white spray paint (it is better to work outside if possible), and then wipe the paint off with a soft cloth to create a "limed" effect. The box must be worked in sections and the paint rubbed off really well. If you want the grain to appear more pronounced, put a little turpentine on the cloth and rub off some more of the paint.

The shell-covered lid is done in the same way; rub off the paint around the lid edge and a few of the shells to expose some of the natural color. Allow the paint to dry.

Apply the gold paint or felt-tip pen to the areas you want to highlight. Allow to dry. Make a useful tab so that it is easier to lift off the lid. Simply gather a small rosette and fasten a pearl bead in the center. Glue the rosette on the lid at one edge, take the ribbon down, and glue the end just inside the lid; allow to dry. Replace the lid with the ribbon hanging on the outside; cut this to make a short tab. Glue the pearl beads over the surface of the box.

Right *The box looks quite opulent and costs so little to make - it will be a permanent and pleasant reminder of trips to the sea.*

Lace-Covered Pillow

A pillow like this will grace any bedroom, its elegance redolent of a bygone age. Use fabric in a gentle subdued shade for the background, and then apply a riot of lace. The pillow is ideal for any scraps of lace you may have collected but have not found a practical use for. You can have a lot of fun playing around with the design before you stitch the lace into position, and then you have the pleasure of presenting it to a good friend as a gift.

Finished size: 14 x 14in (35 x 35cm)

Materials

Two pieces of pale gray cotton, 15 x 15in (38 x 38cm) square
Dressmaker's pins
Lace, at least 10-12 pieces, no less than 15in (38cm) in length and 1¼in (3cm) wide
Two or more lengths of Offray single-face satin ribbon, 15 in (38cm) in length, ⅜in (9mm) wide, in silver gray
Sewing thread, in white and gray
Ruffled white lace, 1¾yd (1.60m) in length, 5½in (14cm) wide
Zipper, 12in (30cm) in light gray
Ready-made square pillow form, 14 x 14in (35 x 35cm)

To make the pillow face piece

Place the square of gray cotton fabric on the work table and begin to pin the strips of lace from the top edge of the pillow, working downward. Move them about to get the best arrangement, perhaps putting a narrow strip over a wide one, or balancing a heavily patterned strip with a less dominant piece.

The lace used for the edging on this pillow will get plenty of handling, so make sure it is not antique lace that could fall apart.

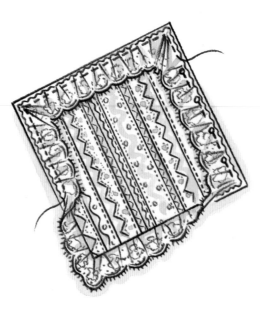

Pin the wide lace trim, facing inward all around the square - after the backing is sewn on, the lace will stand out.

When you have achieved a good arrangement, begin to stitch down the lace strips along their edges, using white sewing thread. Use the gray ribbon to join two similar pieces by stitching it down the middle with a wide zigzag machine stitch and gray sewing thread. Continue until you are satisfied with the effect. Pin the wide lace to the edges of the square, facing inward. Stitch all around.

Making up the pillow cover

Trim excess bits of lace and ribbon from the top and bottom edges where necessary. Then neaten one edge with a close zigzag machine stitch; repeat on one side of the remaining piece of gray cotton fabric.

Pin the zipper along the stitched edges in between the two pieces, matching centers, and stitch. Now stitch all around the pillow pieces, including the opening at either end of the zipper. Open the zipper and turn the pillow cover over, so the right sides are facing inside. Then stitch around the remaining three sides with a seam allowance of 1in (2.5cm). Machine zigzag stitch the three sides to neaten the edges, clip the corners across, and turn right sides out. Insert the pillow form and zipper.

Making a pillow cover from lace scraps

Try to put pieces of lace together that are about the same weight. In addition, if your lace pieces are in varying off-white shades, put them all in a weak solution of bleach. Alternatively, tea-dyeing can look very attractive (see page 24).

Right *Odd pieces of lace are stitched onto a gray background, and the design is completed with lace trim for an enchanting pillow.*

Tulip Picture

This elegant canvaswork picture would grace any hall or study with its formal simplicity. The design is based on the decorations that were popular in Europe at the turn of the century. Simple half cross-stitch is worked in a slightly shiny cotton floss to give richness to the surface of the embroidery.

Finished size: 10¾ x 10¾in (27 x 27cm)

❧

Materials
Canvas, white single thread, 14 holes to the inch,
15 x 15in (38 x 38cm) square
Masking tape or seam binding
DMC coton perlé No 5 in the following colors
and quantities:
Four skeins, cream (shade 712)
Two skeins, gray (shade 844)
One skein, green (shade 320)
Two skeins, rust (shade 301)
One skein, red (shade 521)
One skein, plum (shade 043)
One skein, orange (shade 977)
One skein, blue (shade 799)
Tapestry needle, no. 20
Basting thread
Embroidery frame (optional)
Small embroidery scissors
Clean cloth to keep the work in
Steam iron

❧

Above Classic half cross-stitch is used to work this design, which would also be ideal for making up into a pillow.

Right The striking simplicity and cheerful colors of this embroidered picture will brighten up any wall; the needlepoint is worked in coton perlé to give it a sheen.

To prepare the canvas

To protect your hands and clothes, cover the raw edges of the canvas on all sides with either masking tape or seam binding. Press down firmly if you are using the masking tape, or baste on the seam binding. Mark and baste the centers of the canvas. Mount the canvas into the embroidery frame.

To work the embroidery

The central arrows on the chart should match your basting lines. Each colored square represents one half cross-stitch. The design is worked throughout in half cross-stitch (see Techniques, page 110) with a single strand of coton perlé floss. Start to work the design from the center basting lines, carefully counting and stitching each colored square. You may find it helpful to put a checkmark on the squares of the chart you have completed.

To finish

When the embroidery is finished, remove the masking tape or binding from the canvas edges. With a steam iron, press on the wrong side of the embroidery, or cover it with a damp cloth before pressing, at the same time pulling it gently into shape. If it is very out-of-shape, it needs more drastic blocking treatment.

DMC Coton Perlé

Gray 844
Plum 043
Red 321
Green 320
Blue 799
Rust 301
Orange 977
Cream 712

Floral designs on samplers

Patterns of flowers and foliage have been popular motifs throughout the ages and are to be found in practically every sampler that has been stitched. Whilst flowers can be sewn to look as nature intended, they are mostly used in a more abstract pattern form. Needlecrafters often included flowers in their samplers to give symbolic meaning to their work.

Flowers throughout history

The early pagans associated roses with early love, but to the Christians the rose became the symbol of heavenly or divine love and is often used in conjunction with the Virgin Mary. The carnation has a similar meaning to the rose and generally the two are interchangeable. Other flowers that have become established embroidery motifs over the centuries include marigolds, cowslips, violets, tulips, and the pansy, which is reputed to have been a great favorite of Queen Elizabeth I. Throughout the l8th and 19th centuries flowers were used as purely decorative elements and are often depicted in baskets and urns.

Sources of inspiration

Traditional samplers often feature floral designs that were transferred by drawing freehand and this can give a lively and original approach to your work. Visit galleries and museums for ideas and new inspiration, then experiment at home with different flowers and color combinations. It is always best to work out a motif on paper first; in this way you can check that you are happy with a color scheme and the overall design before committing yourself to fabric.

The secrets of successful samplers

Once you have chosen your design and made a paper layout, there are a few simple rules to consider prior to beginning your embroidery.

1. When cutting the fabric, allow a generous margin for mounting and framing your work.

2. Fold the fabric into four, then press the folds lightly with an iron. Tack along these folds, carefully following the line of the cloth. When you have completed your embroidery these threads will be removed.

3. Find and mark the center of your paper layout, then work a narrow hem around the edge of the material to avoid fraying.

4. Always work from the center of the design. This way you avoid the design falling off the edge of the fabric.

5. When doing counted needlework, it is essential that you check the stitch count at regular intervals, especially in a repeat pattern. Similarly, always refer to your chart regularly to ensure that motifs are positioned correctly.

6. Work threads into the back of the embroidery. When you have used up one length of thread, work the end into the back of the work, making sure that it is not seen at the front. Snip the ends of the threads very closely so that they do not show through the cloth.

7. Work with clean hands and do not leave a needle in your work as it may mark the fabric.

Decoupage Hatbox

Bring a hint of yesteryear into your bedroom or dressing room with this sophisticated hatbox - it will keep your favorite hats safe from crushing, damage, and dust. Hatboxes are a practical and appealing way of storing hats, or other items too, because more than one box can be stacked on top of another to save space and create a fabulous display. Making one will not be enough because everybody will want one!

Materials
One hatbox, covered with paper
(it doesn't matter if it is patterned)
Wood alcohol and a rag
Artists' acrylic paint, dark green
Gold felt-tip pen
Small can of clear matt varnish and brush
Floral gift-wrapping paper
Polyvinyl white glue and brush
Turpentine or mineral spirit (to clean brushes)

To paint the box
If the hatbox has a cord, remove it and mark inside the hatbox how it was threaded and where the knots were. Put a little wood alcohol onto the rag and carefully wipe the whole box to remove fingerprints and any traces of grease; this will insure that the paint adheres properly to the surface.

Mix the acrylic paint to a thick, creamy consistency before painting the box. In about an hour, check if any little bits need touching up, especially under the top lid edge. Give the box extra impact by drawing quick, random squiggles with the gold pen over the painted surface. These

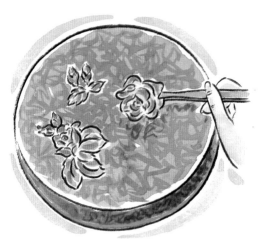

Move the cut-outs around on the lid to find the best arrangement before gluing them down. When you are happy with the design, leave it in place, and pick up and glue each piece separately.

The dotted line indicates the lid position when closed; make sure that your motifs are not glued above it, otherwise they will be half-obscured.

will probably run when you put the final varnish on, and then they can be moved about and spread with the varnish brush to create an interesting effect.

Cut out a motif from your wrapping paper and lay it on the lid to see if the color and size are suitable - you may need to make up a composite image from several pieces. Decide approximately how many motifs you will need to go around the box base, and cut them out.

Apply glue to the back of the motifs and stick them onto the box; press down and rub out from the middle, or use a small roller if you have one. Look at the design to see if it needs something extra - perhaps a few small buds or leaves. Allow the glue to dry thoroughly, checking during the drying time that all the edges of the motifs are stuck down.

To complete the hatbox, give it one - or even two - coats of protective varnish painted on with a brush. Finally, draw a gold line around the bottom edge of the lid and the box. Re-thread the cord, and your box is ready for use.

Other items can be treated in the same way - for example, shoe boxes are easy to come by and perfect for decoupage. Use them for your favorite shoes, or for storing old diaries and odds and ends. Be imaginative when choosing a theme for your decoupage; you could cut out perfume bottles or vintage cars, for example, from magazines. Do not neglect to varnish your decoupage, because this protects the cut-out motifs.

Right The ideal way to keep your best hat in pristine shape and condition is with a decorative hatbox - this one is decoupaged in roses cut from gift-wrapping paper.

Quilted
Patchwork Pillows

LOG CABIN DESIGN

This design developed as an expression of the life of the settlers and pioneers in the early to mid-eighteenth century. They used strips of material salvaged from the clothing and bedding they carried West with them. Pioneer quilt-makers created lovely geometric patterns which represented their cabin homes. In their most simple form these patterns are arranged with a center square of warm red, orange, or yellow fabric to suggest the fire in the hearth and the spirit keeping their faith; the logs (fabric strips) are then placed either side, with the dark strips on one side to show the sadness of life, and the light ones on the other side to suggest happiness. The log cabin patchwork pillow has a quilted center in the shape of the Amish star, so-called after the settlers of that name in Lancaster county, Pennsylvania.

Finished size: approx 21 x 21in (54 x 54cm) square

Materials

*¼yd (20cm) of eight different colors
(four dark, four light)
11in (28cm) square of fabric for center square
22in (56cm) square of batting
22in (56cm) square of backing fabric (muslin)
22in (56cm) square of pillow backing fabric
Scissors
Water-soluble fabric marker
Dressmaker's pins
Basting thread
Quilting thread, Coats and Clark, in rose
Zipper, 20in (51cm)
Sewing thread*

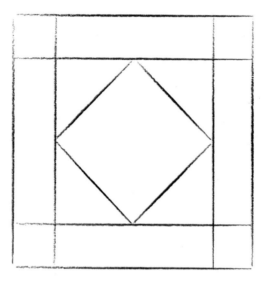

An elegant quilted Amish star as the center diamond in this square design makes an effective pillow pattern.

Position the second strip, and pin and stitch it on to the right-hand edge of the square using the same method as for the first strip. Turn to the right sides and press.

Working the patchwork

Use ¼in (0.6cm) seams throughout. You will be piecing either by hand or by machine through four layers: the two fabrics being pieced together, the batting, and the backing.

The center

Cut out the center square and mark the quilting design (see Techniques, page 116). Trim square to 10¾in (27.3cm). Place a square of batting on top of a 25in (62.5cm) square of muslin (backing fabric). Pin and baste diagonally from corner to corner, each way. Now position the square with the quilting design on it, centered in the middle. Pin and baste in position through all layers.

THE LOGS

The light and dark strips used in the design vary in width, although two consecutive strips are always the same width. Cut out the strips and lay them in your chosen sequence.

Take a light strip for the first log, and place this, right sides down, on one edge of the center quilting square. Cut off excess fabric to fit each time you join a strip. Pin and stitch.

Right *This block design was used by the Amish settlers for their homely quilts. The Amish star motif is featured in the center.*

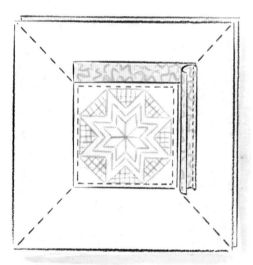

This pattern is one half of the central quilting design. Using tracing paper, draw over the image and repeat it on the opposite side to complete the pattern. Transfer the image to the fabric by placing the tracing paper underneath and drawing onto the fabric with a water-soluble pen.

Turn to the right side and press. Take the next light-colored strip, and pin and stitch it to the right-hand edge of the square in just the same way as before, overlapping the end of the first strip. Work in the same direction each time with the remaining strips.

Quilting the center
Hand-quilt the center with quilting thread. Baste along the outer edges of the pillow front and trim off any excess fabric.

MAKING UP THE PILLOW
Cut the backing fabric to the same depth as the pillow front. Place the pieces right sides together, and baste along one side. Pin the zipper face down on the seam,

matching centers, baste, and stitch. Remove the bastings and open the zipper. Pin and baste the front to the back, right sides together, and stitch all around. Clip the corners and turn right sides out.

DIAMOND IN A SQUARE DESIGN
This design originated with the Amish settlers. Amish religion discouraged frivolity, but their quilt designs were an outlet for individual achievement and love of color. The Amish star in the center is simple and elegant.

Materials
Use ¼in (6mm) seams throughout.
Cream cotton fabric, 11 x 11in
(28 x 28cm) square
Batting, 22 x 22in (56 x 56cm) square
Backing muslin, 22 x 22in (56 x 56cm) square
Pillow backing fabric, 22 x 22in
(56 x 56cm) square
Scissors
Dressmaker's pins
Sewing thread in matching color
Patterned cotton fabric, 10¼ x 10¼in
(26 x 26cm) square, folded diagonally
both ways and cut to make four triangles
Patterned cotton fabric, 8 x 8in (20 x 20cm)
square, folded into four and cut into four squares
Two plain fabric strips,14½ x 4in (37 x 10cm)
Quilting thread, Coats and Clark, in rose
Zipper, 20in (51cm)

To make the diamond in a square design
Mark the quilting design on the center square and make up the layers as before. But this time place the quilting square in the center as a diamond.

The triangles
Cut out four triangles. Place one triangle, right side down, on one raw edge of the diamond. Pin and stitch through all layers, turn to the right side, and press. Repeat by placing the next triangle on the opposite side and continue as before, until all four triangles are stitched in place.

The borders
Pin and stitch small squares of fabric at each end. Pin and stitch these each side of the pillow front. Now pin and stitch the remaining strips to either side. Press.

Quilting the star
Hand-quilt the design in the inner square, as marked.

MAKING THE PILLOW
Follow the instructions for making up a pillow in the Log Cabin Design.

Right Log cabin is a well-known patchwork technique that is popular far and wide. Its graphic simplicity makes it very appealing, especially to beginners.

Girlhood Keepsakes

Pretty items given to girls in their youth tend to be kept through the years, bringing back fond memories of the occasion and the giver. A girl's first sewing basket will keep a budding seamstress arranging and rearranging its contents for hours, even before the first sewing skills are learned. The delightful one featured here, with a needlecase and heart pincushion attached, will endear itself to even the most hardened non-sewer! Padded clothes hangers do a marvelous job of keeping clothes in shape - perhaps the decorative white one with the ribbon bows featured here could hold the little girl's party dress with the dainty tatted collar.

Elegant
Padded Hanger

Padded clothes hangers give a touch of luxury to your wardrobe and also keep clothes in good shape. The lace-edged hanger will help a delicate blouse or dress to stay looking crisp and freshly ironed - although this hanger is almost too pretty to be covered up.

Materials
Medium-thick batting, ½ yd (40cm)
Coat or dress hangers (wooden ones are best),
15in (38cm) in length
Large sewing needle
Matching sewing thread
Paper and pencil
Fabric of your choice, 18 x 11in (46 x 28cm)
Dressmaker's pins
Scissors
In addition, for the dress hanger:
Ruffled lace, ¾in (2cm) wide,
1yd (90cm) in length
Narrow ribbon, ⅜in (9mm) wide,
30in (76cm) in length

Covering the hangers
Cut strips of batting about 3in (7.5cm) wide. Thread the needle with a long length of thread, then begin to wrap batting around the hanger, stitching it down as you go. Don't be afraid to make generous stitches because they will all be covered up in the finished design. It is important, however, to cover the hanger as evenly as possible, without any lumpy areas. Knot the thread really securely.

Cutting out
Draw the hanger shape on a piece of paper; lay your hanger on it and adjust the

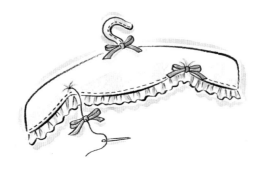

Once the hanger cover is in place over the hook, with its "shoulders" evenly covered, you can secure it through all layers at the points where the ribbon bows are attached.

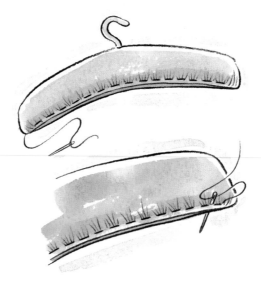

Gather up the lower hem. Then stitch, using small stitches, above the gathering line.

length, if necessary, before cutting out. Fold the fabric with right sides together and place your template on the fold; pin and cut out.

Making up the cover
Place the two cover pieces with right sides together. Pin and stitch around on the dotted line, ½in (1.5cm) from the edge, remembering to "jump" over a stitch where the hook is going to go through. Clip the curves and turn to the right sides.

For the dress hanger
Pin the lace around the edges with right sides together, going up into the curves and making the join at the sides. Stitch and clip the curves, then top stitch ¼in (6mm) from the edge through the lace and fabric layers so they lie flat. Oversew to join the edges of a short length of ribbon for the hook. Pull on the ribbon cover to check if it fits and to assess the length it should be. Finish oversewing to the right length and pull it onto the hook; attach it to the hook base with a few stitches. Cut the ribbon into three pieces. Tie one in a bow around the neck of the hook and stitch it into place. Make the two remaining pieces into neat, even bows, and stitch to the cover at the point where the curves meet, drawing the thread through all layers. Knot the thread securely.

For a sturdy hanger
To give extra support to a heavy garment, you may need to put extra padding on the hanger. This can be done with strips of old, washed pantyhose wound around the wooden hanger before you put the batting on. Alternatively, old shoulder pads taken

from disused garments can be sewn on the ends of the hanger before winding the batting on. Make a cover as before, but with a straight edge at the bottom. Place it over the coat hanger and turn up the hem allowance all around. Gather up as shown in the drawing on page 72 (bottom), using the tiniest of stitches. Then, with matching thread, stitch through to fasten all along the base of the hanger.

To make a sweet-smelling sachet for the hangers

With a small scrap of leftover fabric from the hanger cover and a piece of matching ribbon, you can make a fragrant heart-shaped sachet. Use the template and method for making the little heart pincushion on page 76, but, instead of stuffing, fill with lavender or another sweet-smelling herb - perhaps even a little potpourri. Make a ribbon loop for hanging the sachet over the hook.

Above A special silk blouse will keep its immaculate condition when stored on this luxurious hanger.

Plaid
Sewing Basket

In every family there is a sewing basket or box. Even if there are no great sewers, a sewing basket is a place to store needles, thread, and buttons for those simple repair jobs. This pretty plaid-covered basket is easy to make, with pockets in the sides for the matching needlecase and little pincushion. To prevent scissors and other small items going astray, they can be attached to the inside of the basket with a length of ribbon.

❦

Materials
Basket, roughly 9in (23cm) in diameter,
4in (10cm) deep
Paper and pencil
Plaid taffeta, 1.6yd (1.30m) in length,
45in (115cm) wide
Dressmaker's pins
Scissors
Sewing thread in matching colors
Basting thread
Twill tape for ties (optional)
Offray green ribbon, 1½in (39mm) wide,
2¼yd (2m) in length
Offray red ribbon (shade 260),
¼in (39mm) wide, 2.3yd (2m) in length
Red felt, 6 x 6in (15 x 15cm) square
Green felt, two pieces of 5½ x 3¼in
(14 x 8cm)

❦

To cut the fabric for the basket
Make a paper pattern of the side section from the template featured on page 118. Pin the pattern on a double thickness of fabric and cut out; repeat this method three more times to make four sides.

Cut out two fabric circles for the base, each 7in (18cm) in diameter. Cut a

a piece of fabric for the ruffle, 88½in (225cm), with the stripes of the plaid running downward (widthwise). You may have to join two pieces together to get the right length. Cut four pocket pieces, 5 x 4¼in (12 x 10.5cm).

To make up the lining
All seams are ⅜in (1cm). Pin the side sections and the base pieces right sides

Above The side pockets of the sewing basket can hold scissors, buttons, pin boxes, and a variety of other essential items - everything you need for basic mending and sewing.

Right Sewing baskets should always look like this, with a pretty jumble of the most interesting and useful sewing items spilling out.

Left *Make knife pleats to shape the skirt around the basket - they should touch the table surface. Mark the stitching line with pins.*

Right *A matching heart needlecase and pincushion look very attractive and would make perfect individual gifts.*

together in pairs. From now on treat them as one thickness. Work a loose satin stitch or machine zigzag around the edges of the base circle and sides to prevent fraying. Join side pieces and press open side seams. Fold the base in half and half again, making a small notch at the edge of each corner. Pin base to sides, matching notches and side seams; stitch and press open.

Hem the top of each pocket, turning under ⅝in (1.5cm); press under ⅜in (1cm) on the other sides. Pin each pocket in position, equally spaced, on the sides and stitch ¾in (2cm) from edge. Stitch a dividing line on two of the pockets to contain narrow items.

Join ruffle pieces, pressing the seams open. Make a ⅝in (1.5cm) hem on the lower edge and press. Pleat the ruffle evenly with 1¼in (3cm) knife pleats, pin, and baste. Pin to the top edge of the lining, right sides together, and stitch. Press open. Turn the completed lining over to its underside, and stitch short lengths of twill tape or ribbon to tie through the basket cane to keep the lining firmly in place.

For the top trimming on the basket, make the remaining wide green ribbon into a gathered ruffle. Work a central row of running stitches down the full length of the ribbon and pull up the thread until the gathered ribbon fits the basket edge. Machine-stitch along the center of the ruffle, turning under the ribbon edges to make a neat finish.

Needlecase

From the spare basket lining fabric, cut four pieces 5 x 7¼in (12 x 18cm). Baste them together in pairs. With right sides together, make a ⅜in (1cm) seam around the edges, leaving a 2in (5cm) gap on one long side for turning. Clip the corners, turn right sides out, and press. Turn edges in at the gap and hand-sew along the seamline to close.

With doubled thread, hand-sew a neat line of running stitches about ¼in (0.5cm) in from the edge. Cut out a heart from red felt using the template on page 117, and slipstitch this onto the front cover. Inside the cover, place green "leaves" and pin the center line. Cut a 16in (40cm) length of the red ribbon and place over the inside center line; machine- or hand-stitch down the middle. Fold the case in half and press lightly. Tie the ribbon in a bow and catchstitch it in place.

Heart pincushion

Cut out two hearts using the template, and cut a 14in (35cm) length of red ribbon. Place the two hearts together, and then pin one end of the ribbon in the top center. Oversew with red thread, using close stitches and leaving a small opening for the stuffing. There are many options for filling the pincushion - emery powder is the best because it sharpens your needles every time you push them in; however, it is difficult to find. Well-dried coffee grounds are also good because they prevent needles rusting. Toy stuffing can be used, but it must be pushed in really hard.

When you have stuffed the heart, close up the opening. Stitch on small beads or decorate the heart with gold pen squiggles. Stitch the loose end of the ribbon inside one of the pockets, so it will not get lost. Join small scissors in the same way.

Girl's Tatted Collar

easures 7in (18cm) from the center front to the center back.

Materials

*Coats Mercer-Crochet No.20:
one ball in your selected color
Tatting shuttle
Fine crochet hook
Needle and scissors*

Key to abbreviations:

Sm:	small	cl:	close
R:	ring	prev:	previous
ds:	double stitch	ch/chs:	chain/chains
p/ps:	picot/picots	RW:	reverse work
sep:	separated		

FIRST ROW: This is the foundation row and neck edge of the collar. Tie ball and shuttle threads together.
1. Sm R of 1 ds, 1 sm p, 2 ds, 3 ps sep by 3 ds, 3 ds, cl.
2. Ch of 4 ds.
3. RW. Larger R of 4 ds, 3 ps sep by 4 ds, 4 ds, cl.
4. RW. Ch of 4 ds.
5. R of 3 ds, join to last p of prev sm R, 3 ds, 1p, 3 ds, 1p, 3ds, cl.
6. Ch of 4 ds.
7. RW. R of 4 ds, join to last p on prev larger R, 2 ds, 4 ps sep by 2 ds, 4 ds, cl.
8. RW. Ch of 4 ds
9. R of 3 ds, join to last p on prev sm R, 3 ds, 1p 3ds, 1p, 3 ds, cl.
10. Ch of 4 ds.
11. RW. R of 4 ds, join to last p of prev larger R, 4 ds, 1p, 4ds, 1p, 4ds, cl. Repeat steps 4-11, nine more times.
12. RW. CH of 4 ds.
13. Sm R of 3 ds, join to last p on prev sm R, 3 ds, 1p, 3ds, 1p, 2ds, 1 sm p, 1 ds, cl. Cut and sew in ends.

SECOND ROW: Tie ball and shuttle threads together.
1. R 1 ds, 1 sm p, 3 ds, 1 p, 4ds, join to 2nd p of first larger R on lst row.
2. ds, 1p, 2 ds, 1p, 4ds, cl. 2. RW ch of 5ds, 1p, 6ds, 1p, 5ds. Join by shuttle thread to center p of 2nd larger R on lst row. 5 ds, join to prev p on ch, 6 ds, 1 p, 5 ds.
3. RW. R of 4 ds, 1p, 2ds, 1p, 2ds. Join to p on 3rd larger ring on first row. 2 ds, 1p, 2ds, 1p, 4 ds, cl.
4. RW. Ch of 5 ds, 1p, 6ds, 1p, 5ds. Join to center p of 4th larger R on first row. 5 ds. Join to prev p on ch, 6 ds, 1p, 5 ds.
5. Repeat steps 3 and 4, six (6) more times, joining rings to single picots, and chains to center picots, of larger R on 1st row.
6. RW. R of 4 ds, 1p, 2ds, 1p, 2ds. Join to p on next larger R of first row. 2 ds, 1p, 2 ds, 1p, 4 ds, cl.
7. RW. Ch of 5 ds, 1p, 6 ds, 1p, 5 ds. Join to center picot of next larger ring on 2nd row. 5 ds. Join to prev p on ch. 6 ds, 1p, 5 ds. Miss the next larger ring on 1st row and join to center p of 2nd

last larger R on the first row.
8. Ch of 3 ds, 1p, 3 ds. Join to p on last larger R on 1st row. Cut and sew in ends.

THIRD ROW: Tie ball and shuttle threads together.
1. Join shuttle thread to first (sm) p of first R on 2nd row.
2. RW. Ch of 4 ds, 1 p, 4 ds. Join to first p on first ch on 2nd row.
3. Ch of 3 ds, 3 ps sep by 2 ds, 3ds. Join to last p on first ch of 2nd row.
4. Ch of 3 ds, 5 ps sep by 2 ds, 3 ds. Join to first p of 2nd ch on 2nd row. Repeat step 4 eight 8 more times, joining chs to ps on 2nd row.
5. Ch of 3 ds, 3 ps sep by 2 ds, 3 ds. Join to last p of 6th ch of row 2. Cut and sew in ends.

FOURTH ROW: This is the final row and edging for the collar. Join ball and shuttle threads together.
1. Join shuttle thread to first (sm) p of first R on first row.
2. RW. Ch of 2 ds, 3 ps sep by 2 ds, 2ds. Join to first p of first larger R on first row.
3. Ch of 2 ds, 3 ps sep by 2 ds, 2ds. Join to first p on first R on 2nd row.
4. Ch of 2 ds, 4 ps sep by 2 ds, 2ds. Join to first p on 3rd row.
5. Ch of 2 ds, 7 ps sep by 2 ds, 2 ds.
6. RW. R of 2 ds, 3 ds sep by 1 ds, 2 ds. Join to center p of 2nd

chain of 3rd row. 2 ds, 3 ps sep by 1 ds, 2 ds, cl.
7. RW. Ch of 2 ds, 7 ps sep by 2ds, 2ds.
8. RW. R of 3 ds, 3 ps sep by 1 ds, 3 ds. Join to center p of 3rd ch on 3rd row. 3 ds, 3 ps sep by 1 ds, 3 ds, cl. Repeat steps 7 and 8, eight more times, joining Rs to center ps of chains on 3rd row.
9. RW. Ch of 2 ds, 8 ps sep by 2 ds, 2 ds. Join to center p of last ch on 3rd row.
10. Ch of 2 ds, join to last p on prev ch. 2 ds, 8 ps sep by 2 ds, 2ds. Join to first p on 7th ch of 2nd row. Ch of 2 ds, join to last p on prev ch. 2 ds, 7 ps, sep by 2 ds, 2ds.
11. Join to last p on 7th ch of 2nd row. Ch of 2 ds, join to last p on prev ch, 2 ds, 6 ps sep by 2 ds, 2 ds.
12. Join to first p on 8th ch of 2nd row. Ch of 2 ds, join to last p on prev chain.° 2 ds, 5 ps sep by 2 ds, 2 ds. Join to last p on 8th ch of 2nd row. Repeat from ° 3 more times joining chs to next 3 ps on 1st row.
13. Ch of 2 ds 5 ps sep by 2 ds, 2 ds. Join to last p of last larger R on lst row.
14. Ch of 2 ds, 3 ps sep by 2 ds, 2 ds. Join to last (sm) p of last sm ring on first row.

Cut and sew in ends. Repeat all four rows one more time to make the other half of the collar.
Press lightly. Position the wider ends of the collar pieces together at the center front of dress-neck edge. Slipstitch into place through single picots on small rings of neck edge of collar.

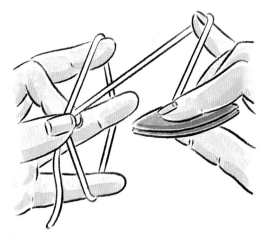

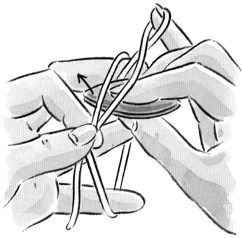

1. Use about 20in (50cm) of thread from shuttle. Hold end between index finger and thumb of left hand. Take thread over 2nd, 3rd, and 4th fingers, then back between thumb and index finger again. (The loop is the ring thread; the shuttle thread runs to the shuttle.)

2. To work first half of double stitch, hold shuttle thread around little finger of right hand. Hold shuttle between thumb and index finger of right hand. Take shuttle under and past both shuttle and ring threads.

3. Now withdraw the shuttle, taking it over the ring thread, but under the shuttle thread. Keep the knot, which is the first half of the double stitch, quite loose around the shuttle.

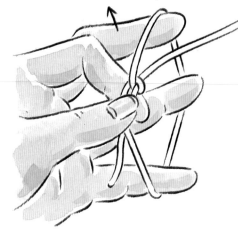

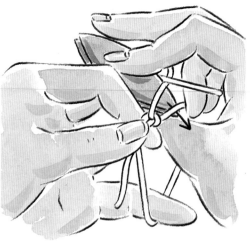

4. Relax fingers slightly, and gently pull the shuttle thread taut until it runs through the stitch on the ring thread. The function of the threads is now reversed and the shuttle thread slips through the knot.

5. The second stage of the double stitch. Still holding the shuttle thread around the little finger of the right hand, take shuttle over and beyond shuttle and ring threads.

6. Withdraw the shuttle, this time taking it under the ring thread and over the shuttle thread. Keep the resulting second half of the stitch loose on the shuttle thread.

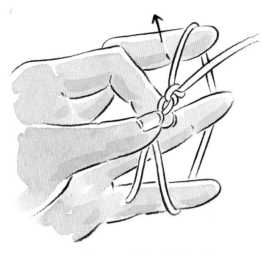

7. Relax the fingers of the left hand very slightly, and gently pull the shuttle thread taut until it runs straight through the completed stitch, which is now on the ring thread. This completes the first double stitch around the ring of thread.

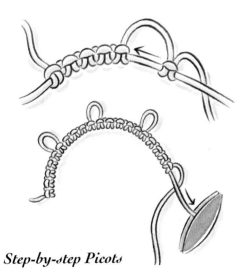

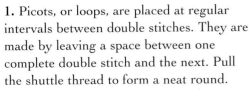

Step-by-step Picots

1. Picots, or loops, are placed at regular intervals between double stitches. They are made by leaving a space between one complete double stitch and the next. Pull the shuttle thread to form a neat round.

2. Picots are used to link rings. Instead of working a picot on the ring, insert the crochet hook in the picot of last ring and draw the thread from last double stitch (ds) through.

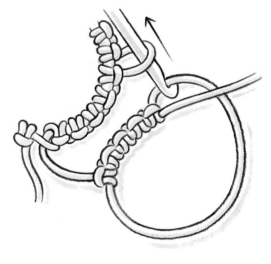

3. Take shuttle through resulting loop and carefully gauge. Do not reverse stitch on to wrong thread. The "join" takes the place of a picot. Subsequent rings are joined to previous one this way.

Childhood Treasures

The most traditional heirlooms come to the fore in this chapter - from an embroidered christening gown to a baby's quilt and a rag doll. Such items are a record of a child's first years and will most likely be kept and treasured, no matter what state of disrepair they may eventually succumb to. The christening gown and quilt can be passed down through the family and used for a second generation of children, and the rag doll is likely to stay a girl's best friend even as she grows older. The friendly duck bag will give a temporary home to many pairs of socks before they reach the laundry, while the stamp box will provide a safe place for a young collector to store interesting and beautiful stamps.

Rag Doll

This doll is sure to become a young girl's best friend. The pattern is simple to make, and changes can be made to her skin color or hair style.

Materials

FOR THE DOLL
Paper and pencil
9 x 45in (25 x 115cm) cream cotton or polyester-cotton fabric
Scissors
Child-safe synthetic stuffing
Ball of dark brown sportweight yarn
Cream and brown sewing thread
Stranded embroidery floss, in black, dark brown, coral, red, pale blue, and pale pink
Small embroidery hoop (optional)

FOR THE CLOTHES
¼yd (20 x 115cm) gray and white, narrow-striped cotton fabric
¼yd (20 x 115cm) gray and white, wide-striped cotton fabric
8in (20cm) square of white cotton fabric
18in (50cm) narrow, ruffled eyelet
39in (1m) narrow lace
6in (15cm) narrow elastic
1in (2cm) white fusible fabric
Length of red Offray ribbon, ⅛in (3mm) wide
Small piece of red felt for the shoes

Making the Rag Doll

Make paper patterns from the templates, allowing ¼in (5mm) extra all around for the seams. Take the cream fabric and lay the pattern pieces on top of the straight grain of the fabric. Cut out one body piece and mark the outline and features on another, but don't cut it out. Now cut out four leg pieces and four arm pieces.

The Rag Doll's face is very calm and gentle – small delicate stitches are used to create her fine features.

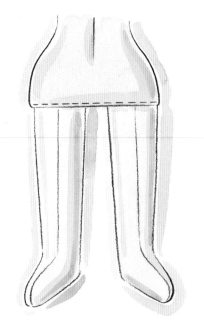

Turn in the seam allowance at the base of the body. Then insert the legs with the center seams facing forward, pin, and stitch.

Making the arms and legs

Stitch all around, leaving the top edge open. Turn to the right sides. Stuff firmly in the lower half and quite loosely in the top half. Turn in edges and baste across.

Embroidering the face

Work as follows with two strands of embroidery floss in the needle:
eyebrows - stem stitch in dark brown
eyelids - backstitch in dark brown
eyelashes - straight stitch in dark brown
eyeballs - satin stitch in black and very pale blue
nose - two backstitches in coral
cheeks - satin stitch in pale pink
lips - backstitch outline and satin stitch in coral; the line between lips - backstitch in red (see Techniques, page 101–103, for instructions on working the stitches).

Making the body

Cut out the embroidered body piece. Make the dart on both body pieces on the wrong side, pin, and stitch. With right sides together, pin the two body pieces together, inserting the arms inside the body. Stitch around the edges, but leave an opening; clip the curves and turn right sides out. Stuff the head and body very firmly. Pin the legs into position, turning in the edges of the body at the same time; stitch across.

Putting on the hair

To make the hair, cut 50 pieces of brown knitting yarn 12in (30cm) long. Holding the lengths next to one another, make a parting by machine-stitching down the center with brown thread. Pin the hair to the doll's head and stitch it down along the parting. Draw the ends of the hair to the back, into a bun.

Making the doll's clothes

Make paper patterns from the templates on page 121. Cut out the pattern pieces from the fabric for the bodice, sleeves, pantalets, and shoes. From the wide, striped cotton, cut a skirt piece 18 x 4 ½in (46 x 11cm) and a skirt ruffle in narrow-striped cotton 26 x 3 ½in (66 x 9cm).

Blouse

Stitch lace to the sleeve edge and make tiny pleats at the shoulder edge. Matching the centers of the shoulders, pin and stitch the sleeve tops to the bodice. Sew the side and the sleeve seams. Stitch the lace down the right front edge and around the neck, turning in a hem along the left front edge. Finish with a red ribbon bow.

Pantalets

Stitch lace along the bottom edges. Stitch center seams. Place back and front together, right sides facing, and stitch around the leg seam. Make a hem at the waist for the elastic; stitch, leaving a small gap. Thread in the elastic and pull up to fit the doll's waist; secure with a knot.

Skirt

With right sides together, stitch the eyelet ruffle to the lower edge of the large rectangle. Stitch the back seam, stopping 3in (7cm) from the top. Join the back seam of the ruffle and make a narrow hem along one edge. Gather the top edge and stitch to the bottom edge of the skirt. Cut the waistband to fit, and add 1in (2cm) for turnings and overlap. Gather the top edge, then pin and stitch onto the waistband. Turn the waistband to the inside; stitch in place. Turn the waistband to the inside, folding the raw edges in, and stitch neatly in place.

Shoes

For each shoe, stitch two pieces together, leaving the top open.

Right This Edwardian-style Rag Doll is soft and comforting to hold.

Baby's Quilt

The arrival of a new baby is the perfect excuse to make this crib quilt.

Finished size: 39 x 49in (99 x 124cm)

Materials
Semi-transparent graph layout paper
Black felt-tip pen
Two pieces of white polyester-cotton fabric,
48 x 39in (122 x 99cm)
14in (35cm) dark pink, patterned, cotton fabric,
46in (115cm) wide
14in (35cm) light pink, patterned, cotton fabric,
46in (115cm) wide
10in (25cm) light green cotton fabric,
46in (115cm) wide
4in (10cm) dark green cotton fabric,
46in (115cm) wide
Spool each of pink and green cotton thread
10in (25cm) lightweight fusible interfacing
Basting thread
Two spools of quilting thread
2oz piece of batting, 48 x 39in (122 x 99cm)
Water-soluble pen
Quilting frame (optional)

To make the design
The template is just one-quarter of the quilt, so it will need to be repeated. Start by enlarging the quarter design on a photocopier to the actual size, 19 ½ x 26in (50 x 66cm). Make the mirror image by placing graph paper over the quarter pattern and drawing over it with a black felt-tip pen. Lay them side by side and stick together with clear tape. Transfer the design to the white fabric by placing the paper underneath and lightly tracing with a water-soluble pen. Repeat to obtain the whole design.

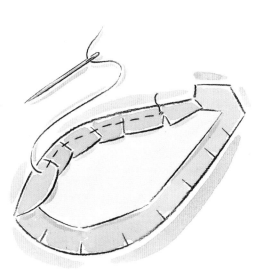

Each motif is folded over the edges of the fusible interfacing after clipping the curves. Then an even line of basting stitches is worked around the shape to hold it in place.

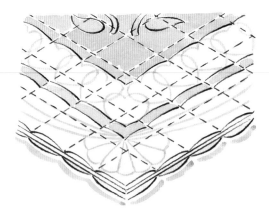

Once the appliqué has been applied, a grid of basting stitches is worked over the whole quilt through all layers to hold them in place before quilting.

Triangles and narrow border
Cut four triangles in dark pink, patterned fabric with 12in (31cm) sides; turn under ¼in (5mm) all around and slipstitch.

For the light green border, cut four strips 18 x 1 ¼in (45 x 3cm) in length and two strips 32 x 1 ¼in (78 x 3cm) in length. Press a ¼in (5mm) turning along both edges and slipstitch in place.

Stems
Cut 12 bias strips in light green fabric, each one 10 x 1in (25 x 2.5cm). Fold in half lengthwise and machine- or hand-stitch with running stitches close to the edge. Press stems and slipstitch in place.

Flowers and leaves
Make paper templates for the flowers and leaves, tracing the motifs on page 122. Cut out the flower shapes, inner flowers, and center circles, four of each in dark pink, patterned fabric and four of each in light pink, patterned fabric. Cut out 24 leaves, 12 of each shape - six in dark green and six in light green. Draw around the templates onto the interfacing - cut out 24 leaves, eight flowers, eight inner flowers, and eight center circles. Press the interfacing shapes onto the matching fabric shapes. Stitch alternate-colored flowers in place.

Quilting and finishing
Assemble the quilt top on the backing fabric with the batting sandwiched between. Work a 4in (10cm) grid of basting stitches. To quilt, work small, even running stitches on the lines. Cut 2 ¾in (7cm) bias strip in light pink, patterned fabric, and join on the diagonal to make a length of 174in (445cm). Stitch to the quilt top. Fold over to the back and slipstitch.

Dorothy
Duck Bag

Little children will remember to put their socks away if they have a friendly duck hanging on their door! The more she is filled, the wider her wings spread out, so you know when to empty her!

❧

Materials
Paper and pencil
⅝yd (½ m), 36in (90cm) wide, printed cotton fabric
Dressmaker's scissors
Dressmaker's pins
Two squares of yellow felt, 12¼in (31cm)
Square of orange felt, 12¼in (31cm)
Small pieces of white and black felt
Matching sewing thread
Small amount of child-safe stuffing
White cotton fabric, 10in (25cm)
⅝yd (50cm) ruffled eyelet or lace
Narrow ribbon, 12in (30cm)

❧

To make the Dorothy Duck Bag
Cut two 17¼in (44cm) squares from the printed cotton fabric. Place right sides together, and cut off a triangle 2¼in (6cm) deep at both top and bottom points. Cut a facing strip 14 x 4in (35 x 10cm); turn under the edges to neaten. Stitch the facing in place, then cut down the middle and clip the corners. Turn the facing to the other side and stitch ¾in (2cm) from the opening all the way around.

Place the two pieces of the bag together, right sides facing, and stitch side seams.

Head and feet
Trace the patterns onto paper and cut out. Pin the head and feet shapes onto the yellow felt, and cut out two heads and four

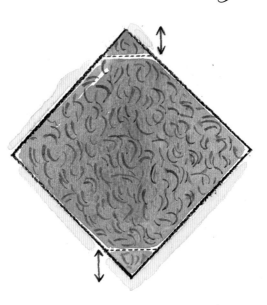

Cut off the top and bottom points from both squares of fabric.

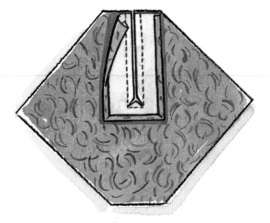

Position the facing for the front opening and then stitch carefully around the edge before clipping the corners inward.

feet. Cut out two beak pieces from the orange felt, then cut out two white eyes with two black centers in felt.

Place the head pieces together and oversew all around, from one bottom neck edge to the other. Stuff firmly, then stitch to close the base of the neck. Place the upper beak onto the lower one, and oversew all the way around up to the marked "v." Stuff lightly, and then stitch the beak onto the head.

Pin the large white eyes and the black centers in position on the head, and stitch in place. Place the two pairs of feet together and stitch all around the outer edge. Stuff lightly, and then stitch the lines through all thicknesses.

Turn in a hem at the top edge of the bag. Make a row of running stitches and gather around the neck of the duck. Now turn in a small hem at the bottom edge of the bag and insert the feet; stitch across securely.

Bonnet and collar
Cut a circle 9½in (24cm) from the white cotton fabric; fold it in half and cut across. Stitch the eyelet around the edge of one half. Neaten the straight edge with a small hem and baste a line along the top edge. Pull up the thread to gather the back.

Place the bonnet on the head and pin; push in a small amount of stuffing to fill the bonnet back. Pleat the back of the bonnet into the head and secure. Fold the remaining half-circle in two and cut across. Stitch eyelet onto the lower edge of one quarter, turn under the top edge, and wrap around the neck with the join at the back; stitch in place. Fold the ribbon for the loop in half and pin to the back of the head. Stitch securely from the neck up to the bonnet back.

Right *Dorothy Duck will always keep a friendly eye on children's laundry, while they will make her wide wings spread out as they stuff in their socks. The design is based on my memory of a duck that used to hang on my great-grandmother's kitchen door.*

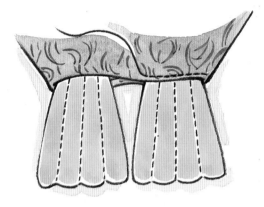

Turn in the hem allowance, insert the feet, and then stitch across.

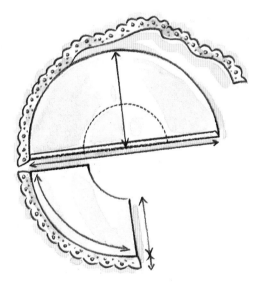

Stitch on the lace trim, then cut away the top half of the circle to make the bonnet.

89

Embroidered Christening Gown

The birth of a baby is an event to celebrate, and the christening is the time for family and friends to get together to welcome the new arrival. In the past, christening gowns were handed down from one generation to the next. You may be lucky enough to have inherited a family christening gown, but, if you haven't, or if the gown is too small - today, babies tend to be larger - we have devized various ways of customizing a christening set. Of course, you can use these techniques on any dress or outfit for a child, and you may like to look out for antique dresses at flea markets or secondhand clothes stores, as these can often be renewed with attractive decoration.

Materials
Christening set
Matching threads
Embroidery hoop
Matching silk or stranded embroidery floss
Small, sharp scissors
Dressmaker's pins
Matching lace
Seed pearl beads
Buttons

To make the Christening Gown

You can buy either a plain christening set or make your own using a commerical pattern. If you are making your own, remember to use the softest, finest fabrics possible, because babies have delicate, sensitive skin. If you will be doing heavy embroidery on the cotton, you may need to use two thicknesses, or you may choose to back it with a lightweight interlining.

Work any heavy embroidery before assembling the pieces, but, if you are customizing a christening set, you can embroider directly onto the fabric, using an embroidery hoop to hold it taut.

The bodice of the gown pictured here is decorated with tiny pin tucks in vertical

Above Small, satin booties are available in many baby boutiques and can be customized. Remove any superfluous bows or trims, and then sew on your own lace and embroider the booties.

Right A christening gown is truly an heirloom gift to pass down through generations to children and grandchildren.

rows, and the space between the pin tucks is filled with satin-stitched hearts and flowers. The whole bodice panel is trimmed with pretty narrow lace. You may like to repeat the hearts and flowers embroidery on the edges of the dress - depending upon its design, you could decorate around the sleeves, collar, and hem. Sew tiny beads onto the sleeves in a random pattern; trim the sleeves and cuffs with lace.

Here, pleats were added to the bottom of the dress to shorten it, and buttons and loops for closing the dress at the back were sewn on instead of standard buttonholes.

Below Accessories, such as a muslin or voile bonnet and booties, can also be customized.

Right White-on-white embroidery can be used to add beautiful, decorative touches to all pieces of a christening set.

Papier-Mâché
Cottage Coin Bank

A coin bank is an ideal way to teach and encourage children to save money - they will enjoy sending coins down the chimney of this country cottage.

Finished size: 5 x 4in (12.5 x 10cm) at the base, 5½in (14cm) in height

Materials
Tracing paper and pencil
Sheet of ¹⁄₁₆in (1½mm) mediumweight board or cardboard, 17¾ x 17¾in (45 x 45cm)
Straight edge and cutting board
Craft knife
Strong contact glue
Polyvinyl white glue
Masking tape
Sheet of newsprint
Wallpaper paste
Sheet of tissue paper
Acrylic or poster paints, in white, brown, blue, red, and green

To make the Cottage Coin Bank
Trace the pattern pieces for the house, cut them out, and draw around each one onto the board. Use the cutting board and craft knife to cut them out accurately. Score lines as shown on the templates (see pages 125-126), and fold gently.

Make the house base piece into an open box, using strong contact glue on the side tabs to stick them on the inside. Assemble the chimney using both masking tape and strong contact glue to join the pieces. Fit the chimney into the hole in the folded roof; just 2in (4cm) should protrude. Attach the chimney to the inside of the roof with masking tape.

The constructed door has board strips glued together on the right-hand side - these form a finger grip when the door is in the frame.

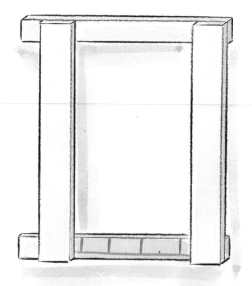

The door frame has a construction of board strips standing free from the house, and the door slides freely behind it. An illusion of the door extending to the ground is made by painting on top of the bottom of the frame.

Making the sliding door
Glue two C strips to the area marked on the door with the dotted line. With strips A and B, make a frame for the door to slide in and out of. Glue the top and bottom of one B strip to two A strips, making sure the edges are flush to create neat right angles. Try the door to make sure that it slides in and out easily. Glue the A pieces above and below the door hole, but do not glue the B strip down to the house base.

The second B strip should now be glued to the frame, so it lies along the line of the door. Only glue the top and bottom of the B strip. Try the door once more to see if it slides easily, then leave it in place.

Covering with papier-mâché
Cut off or tear small pieces of newsprint, about ¾-1in (2½-3cm) wide. Mix up a small amount of wallpaper paste, and dip your finger in the paste to cover the paper.

The roof
For the papier-mâché on the roof, you need some larger pieces of newsprint. Place each paste-covered piece on the roof and push it about with your fingers until it makes a scrunched up texture. To make the texture of the thatching, score and fold the cut-out board shapes and place them on the roof top.

Paint the house in your chosen colors.

Right *The door of the bank will slide open to allow coins to be shaken out.*

Stamp Box

A junior stamp collector would be thrilled to have this box for keeping particularly special stamps in. Likewise, adults will appreciate a home for current postage stamps so they are easy to find. It need not cost very much to make the box, and the technique is simple. The stamps you select for decorating the box could have a theme, such as birds and animals - you can buy a wide range of themed stamp collections from most philatelic shops.

Materials
A shallow, wooden box, such as a cigar box
Stamps, presoaked to remove any paper
Polyvinyl white glue
Brush
Craft knife
Clear spray varnish

To make the Stamp Box
If there are any labels on the box, they must be removed by wetting with a cloth until they can be peeled off. Do not immerse the box in water because it might buckle. Allow the box to dry thoroughly.

Lay out the stamps on a shallow tray or large plate, each one facing upward. Put some polyvinyl glue in a saucer and a sheet of clean paper by the side. Apply glue to the back of each stamp before sticking onto the box. If you find that the first two or three stamps you stick down are lifting, brush the box with glue before sticking on the rest of the arrangement.

Start by gluing the stamps around the edges of the box, taking them over the opening. Work carefully at the corners,

Stamps are beautiful, miniature works of art, that are best seen through a magnifying glass in order to really appreciate them.

When the stamps are thoroughly dry, open the box. Cut along the opening at the hinge with a sharp craft knife, making gentle sawing movements to insure a crisp, even line through the stamps all the way around.

making sure that the stamps are stuck down firmly. Save one or two favorite stamps for the last areas to be filled, to make sure that they show up well.

Leave to dry before checking that each stamp is stuck down securely. Start to release the lid by cutting into the opening at the back near the hinges (if there are any) with a craft knife. Cut slowly and carefully all around until the lid opens; check for rough pieces hanging off the edges and pare these away.

Apply spray varnish in a clean, dry place. Place the box with the lid closed on a jelly jar. Spray one side, then move the box around by putting your finger underneath it and pushing gently without getting your hands sticky. Continue spraying until all sides are coated; leave to dry in a dust-free place.

This collage technique can be used on all sorts of containers and boxes, to make their appearance suit their purpose. For instance, new seed packets could be kept in a box covered in colorful pictures cut from empty seed packets. In addition, a keen wine connoisseur would appreciate a box decorated with wine labels.

Right A treasured stamp collection will be passed down in the family, and will be especially valued if it is kept in a personalized box like this one.

Techniques

All the stitches and sewing techniques you need
to know to create the projects in the book are
clearly explained on the following pages. By
following the clear diagrams and referring to
the accompanying instructions, you will be able to
make up designs successfully, and you will expand
your general sewing know-how in the process.

Satin Stitch

Satin stitch is a filling stitch, consisting of laying threads side by side in a given shape. It takes practice to get the surface smooth and the edges even.

Ladder Stitch

A wide line stitch, ladder stitch is worked downward along two parallel lines and consists of a sequence of crossing stitches, which form the rungs.

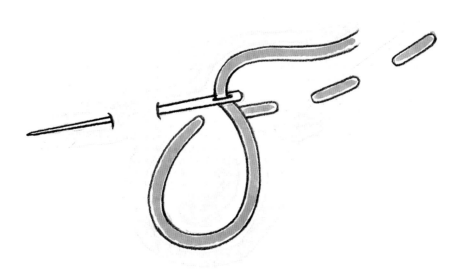

Running Stitch

This is a line stitch with many different uses: as an outline stitch, as a foundation row for more complex stitches, and for hand-quilting.

Work the stitch by passing the needle in and out of the fabric at regular intervals.

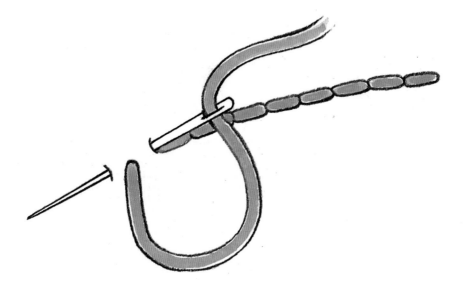

Backstitch

A straight stitch, backstitch often forms the basis for other decorative stitches, especially in blackwork.

Bring the thread through on the stitch line, then take a backward stitch through the fabric. Now bring the needle through a little in front of the first stitch and take it back to reinsert it in the hole formed by the previous stitch. All the stitches should be the same length.

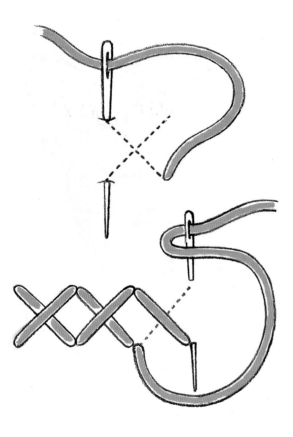

Cross-stitch

This is probably the oldest and best known of all embroidery stitches. It is also very versatile because it can be worked on any fabric or canvas.

There are different methods of working this stitch, depending on the choice of material, but one rule prevails - the top diagonal stitch must always face in the same direction.

To make a single cross-stitch, bring the thread through at the lower right-hand side and insert the needle two threads up (or the required number of threads for a smaller or larger stitch) and two threads to the left, bringing it two threads down to form a half cross. Insert the needle two threads up and two threads to the right to complete the cross.

Chain Stitch

Chain stitch can be used as an outline stitch, or in close rows as a filling. Bring the needle out and hold the thread down with the thumb, then insert the needle through the same hole and bring it out below the first one, keeping the thread under the needle point. Repeat by taking the needle back into the same hole from which it came, holding the thread down with the thumb. Continue like this until you have completed your line; secure with a small, tying stitch.

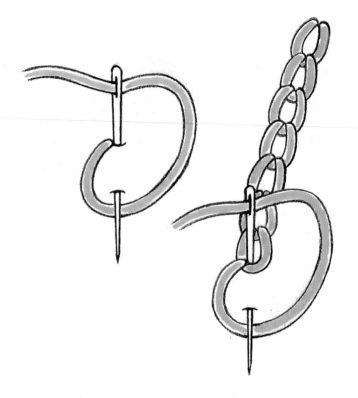

Slipstitch

An invaluable stitch, this is used for hemming and for joining two folded edges. It is also used for attaching appliqué motifs to a surface, in which case the stitches should be as small and invisible as you can possibly make them.

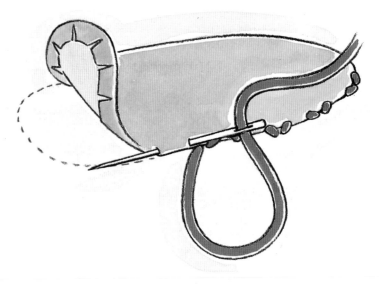

French Knot

A French knot is an isolated stitch with a neat, raised appearance. It has many uses, because it can be worked singly as an accent stitch, massed as a textured area, or used to create a soft outline.

Bring the thread through the fabric in the exact place you want to make the knot. Circle the thread around the needle twice and, holding the thread firmly with your thumb, insert the needle through the fabric close to where you first brought it out. Hold the knot down with your thumb and pull the thread out at the back, securing with a small stitch.

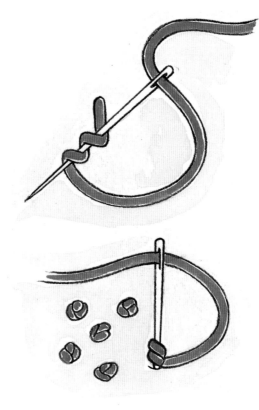

Quilting stitch

The needle is inserted vertically through all layers of fabric and comes up vertically at a measured distance.

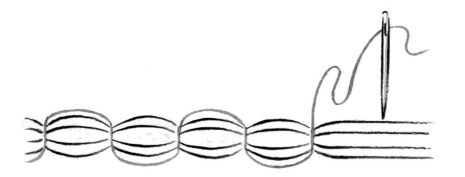

Transferring a Quilting Pattern

You can draw the pattern directly onto the fabric from a printed image, but a sure and easy way to transfer a pattern is to use dressmaker's tracing paper. Choose the paper in a color nearest to your fabric color. Then place it on top of the fabric, which, in turn, is placed on top of the image to be transferred. Hold all three layers in place with strips of masking tape. Then, with a blunt-ended instrument, such as a ballpoint pen, mark out the pattern - preferably with dots rather than a heavy line. Avoid pressing down anywhere other than on the pen because this could make smudges on the fabric.

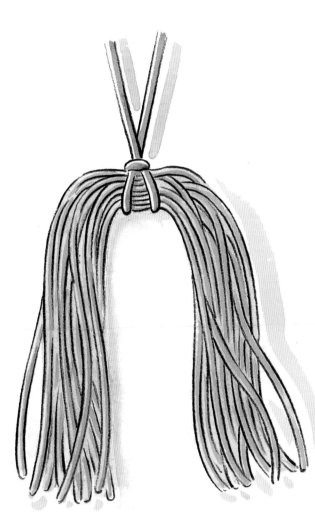
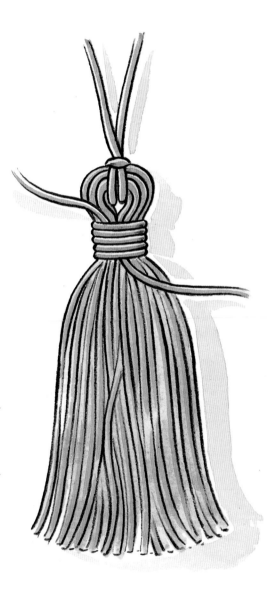

Making a Tassel

Place the cut lengths for the tassel together and fold in half; double over a length of thread, then insert it through the fold and pull tight. Wrap the thread around the tassel just below its head to cover the loose end. Thread the remaining end into a needle and take it into and under the head to secure; cut off.

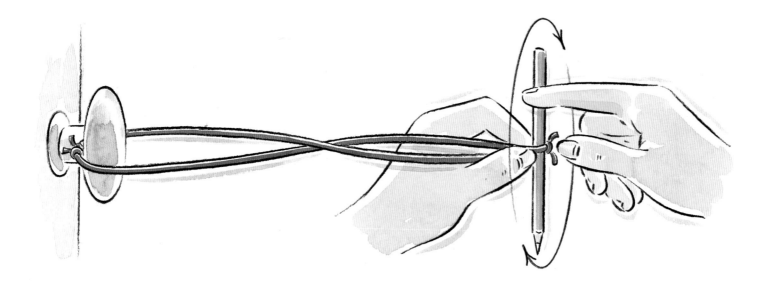

Making a Twisted Cord

Put the knotted strands of thread or floss over a doorknob, insert a pencil at the other end, and twist clockwise until the strands are tightly twisted. Remove from the doorknob, quickly fold in half, and allow to twist together. Pull gently to even out the twists and knot both ends of the cord before using.

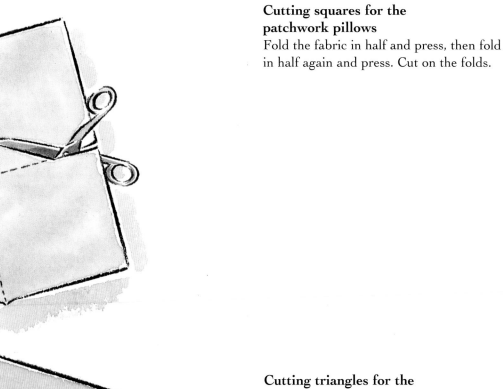

Cutting squares for the patchwork pillows
Fold the fabric in half and press, then fold in half again and press. Cut on the folds.

Cutting triangles for the patchwork pillows
Fold into a triangle and press. Fold again into a smaller triangle and press. Cut on the foldlines.

Cutting Bias Strips

Straighten the fabric edges by cutting or pulling a thread from the fabric and then cutting along it. Fold the fabric diagonally and press firmly. Cut along the foldline and remove one triangle of fabric. Measure and mark along the cut edge to make the strips the width you require. Cut as many strips as you need from both triangles, and join them along the straight grain.

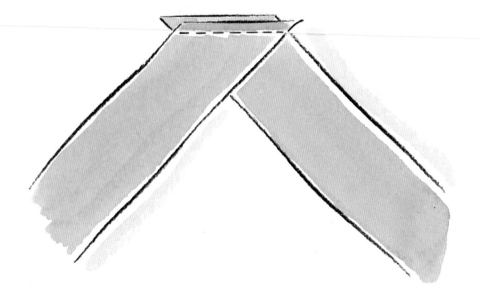

Joining Bias Strips

Place together and join on the straight grain, then press the seam allowance back.

Blocking and pressing

This finishing technique restores the shape of the fabric and removes creases. If the work has been done by hand, the fabric may need to be reshaped quite drastically. Even if it has been worked on a frame, some final shaping is often beneficial.

If the work requires only fine creases to be removed, then a light pressing on the back will be enough. However, if the work is puckered, then it will need to be wet-blocked.

To wet-block surface embroidery:

Attach a piece of blotting paper, larger than the work, to a board with strips of masking tape. Immerse the work in water and squeeze out excess, then place over the blotting paper, right side up. Use thumbtacks or nails to pull it into shape and get it exactly straight. Leave until the work is very dry - this could take a week.

To wet-block canvaswork:

Mark the outline of the size of the work to be blocked on a board, then attach a slightly larger piece of blotting paper with strips of masking tape. Place the work face down if the stitched surface is flat, and face upward if it is textured. Spray with water or dampen with a cloth. Then pull it into shape with thumbtacks or nails. Now wet the work thoroughly and leave until it is really dry before taking it off the board.

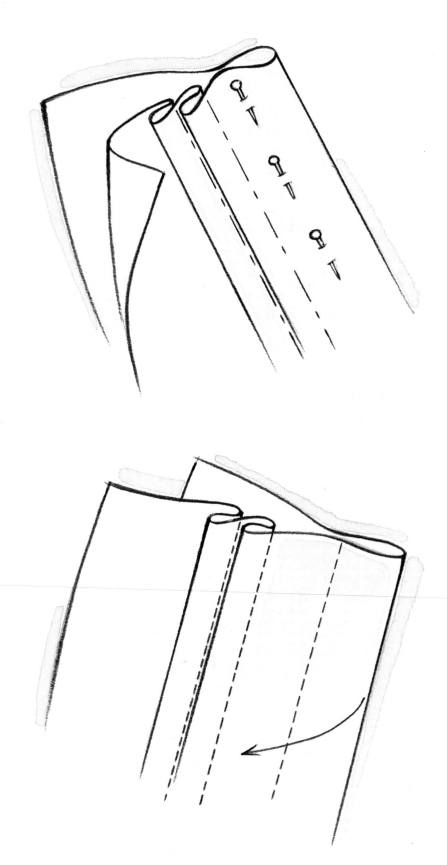

Tucks

Making tucks on the right side of the
fabric adds a decorative touch to clothes –
for example, they may be placed vertically
or horizontally across a bodice or yoke.
Some tucks are stitched down their full
length; others are only partly stitched and
can be used, like darts, to shape a garment.

To add tucks to a garment, make pleats
in the fabric in the width required; pin,
baste, and press before stitching. Pull the
basting threads out and the loose sewing
threads through to the back; thread each
one separately through a needle and run it
back through the stitching for 1in (2.5cm)
before cutting off.

Templates

Wedding Album Cover, pages 22–23

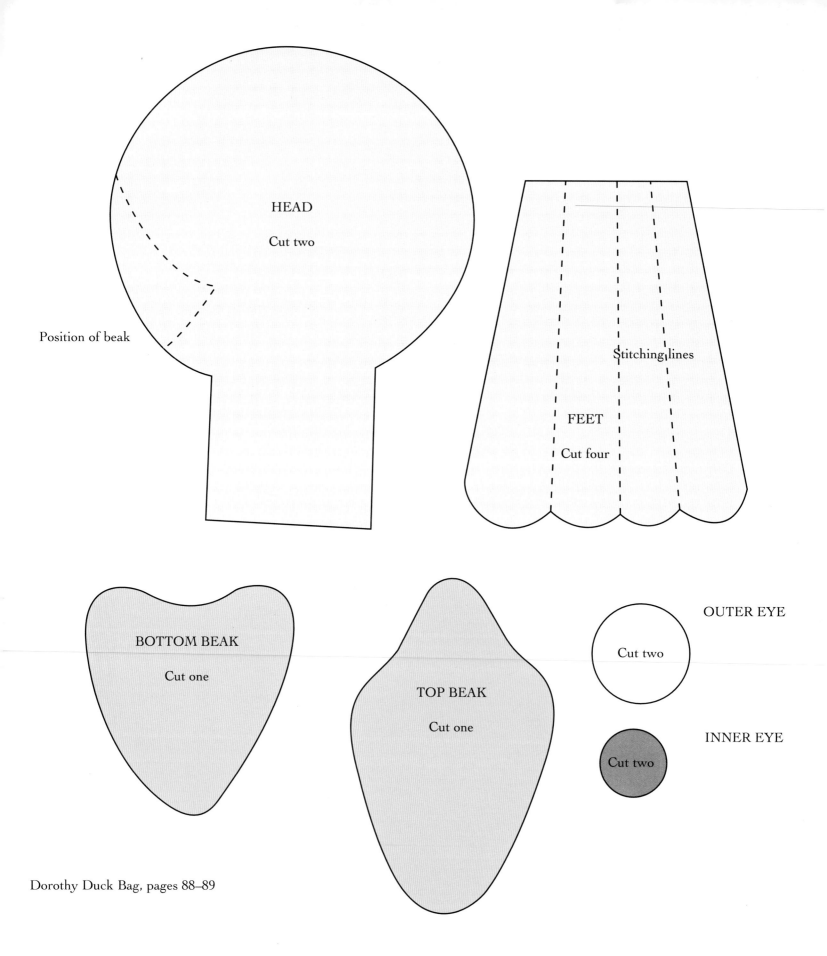

HEAD

Cut two

Position of beak

FEET

Cut four

Stitching lines

BOTTOM BEAK

Cut one

TOP BEAK

Cut one

OUTER EYE

Cut two

INNER EYE

Cut two

Dorothy Duck Bag, pages 88–89

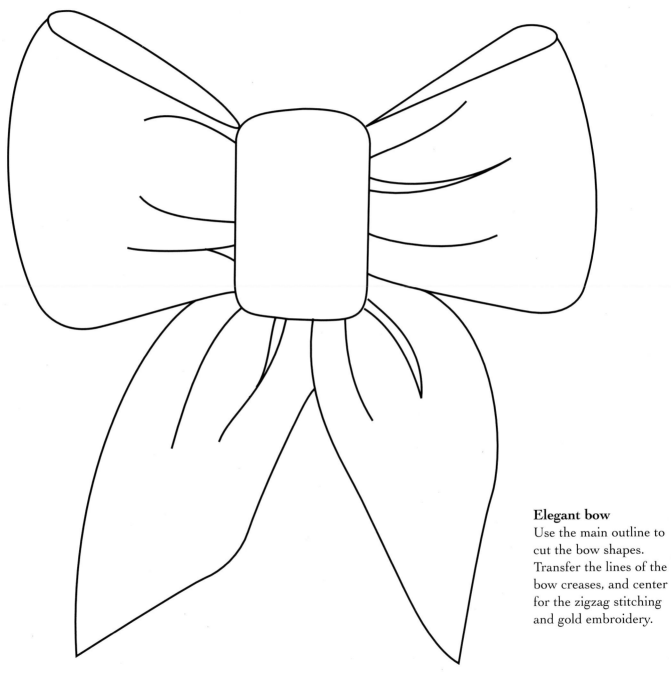

Elegant bow
Use the main outline to cut the bow shapes. Transfer the lines of the bow creases, and center for the zigzag stitching and gold embroidery.

Tablecloth & Napkins, pages 42–43

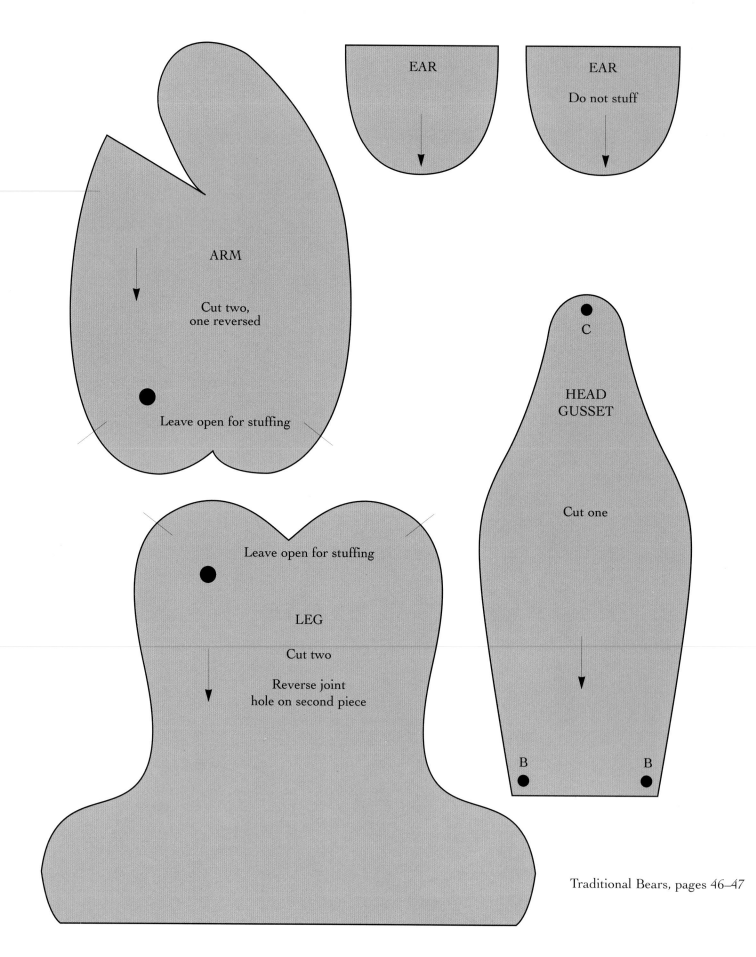

ARM

Cut two,
one reversed

Leave open for stuffing

EAR

EAR

Do not stuff

HEAD
GUSSET

C

Cut one

B   B

LEG

Leave open for stuffing

Cut two

Reverse joint
hole on second piece

Traditional Bears, pages 46–47

Leave gap
for head joint

Leave
open for
stuffing

● Arm joint

BODY

Cut two,
one reversed

Leg joint
●

NOSE
and
MOUTH

NECK CIRCLE

Cut one

EAR

Do not stuff

SIDE HEAD

Cut two,
one reversed

Leave
open for
stuffing

EAR

FOOT PAW PAD

Cut two in felt

ARM PAW PAD

Cut two in felt

Traditional Bears, pages 46–47

This pattern is one half of the central quilting design. Using tracing paper, draw over the image and repeat it on the opposite side to complete the pattern. Transfer the image to the fabric by placing the tracing paper underneath and draw onto the fabric with a water-soluble pen.

Center line

Quilted Patchwork Pillows, pages 66–69

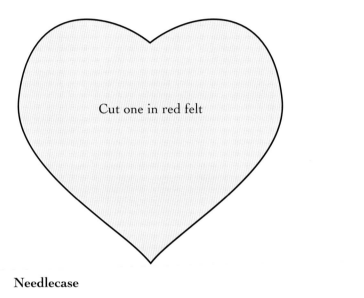

Cut one in red felt

Needlecase

Cut two in red felt

Leave open for stuffing

Pincushion

Sewing Basket, pages 74–77

Basket lining

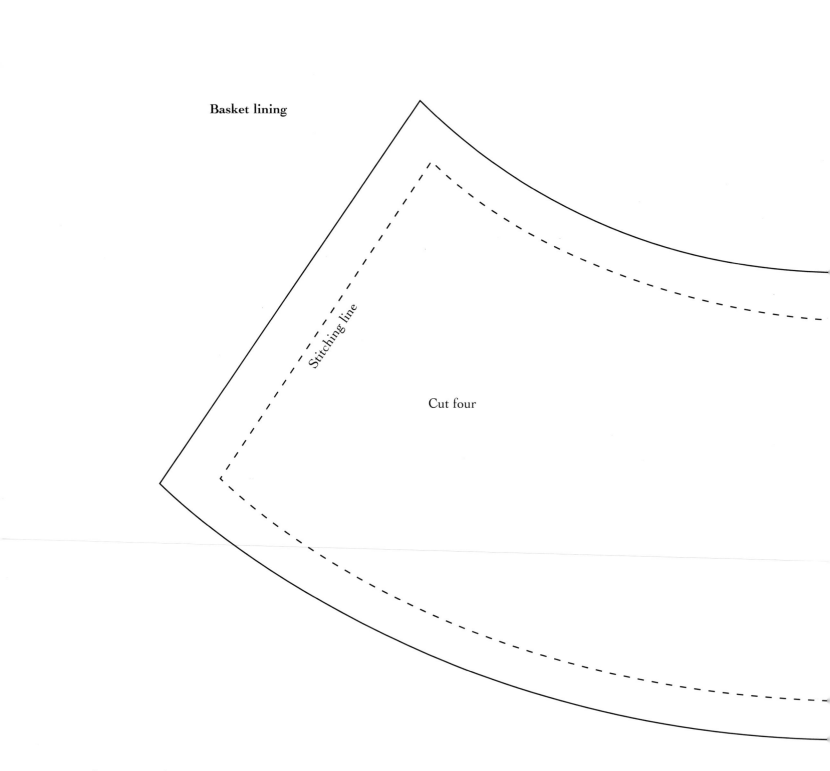

Stitching line

Cut four

Sewing Basket, pages 74–77

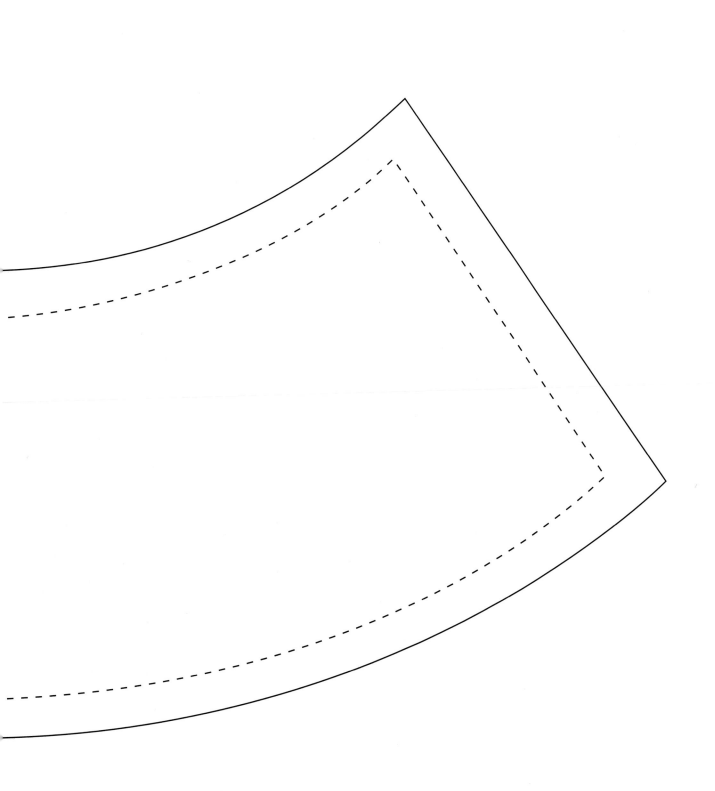

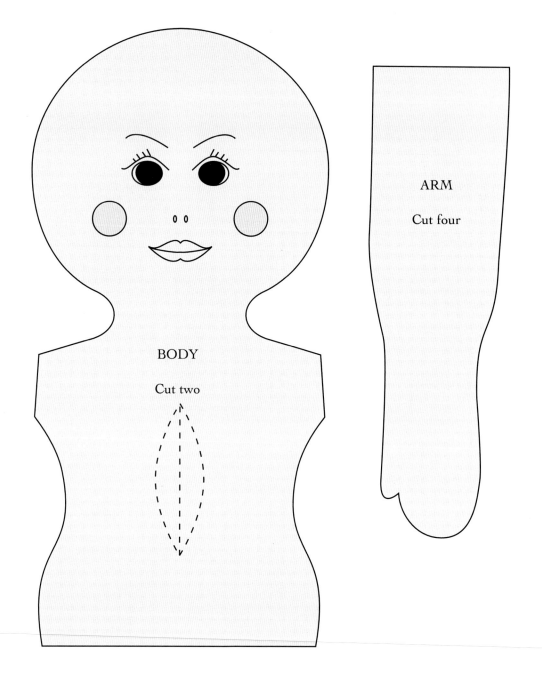

ARM

Cut four

BODY

Cut two

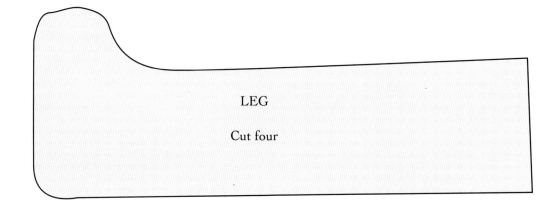

LEG

Cut four

Rag Doll,
pages 84–85

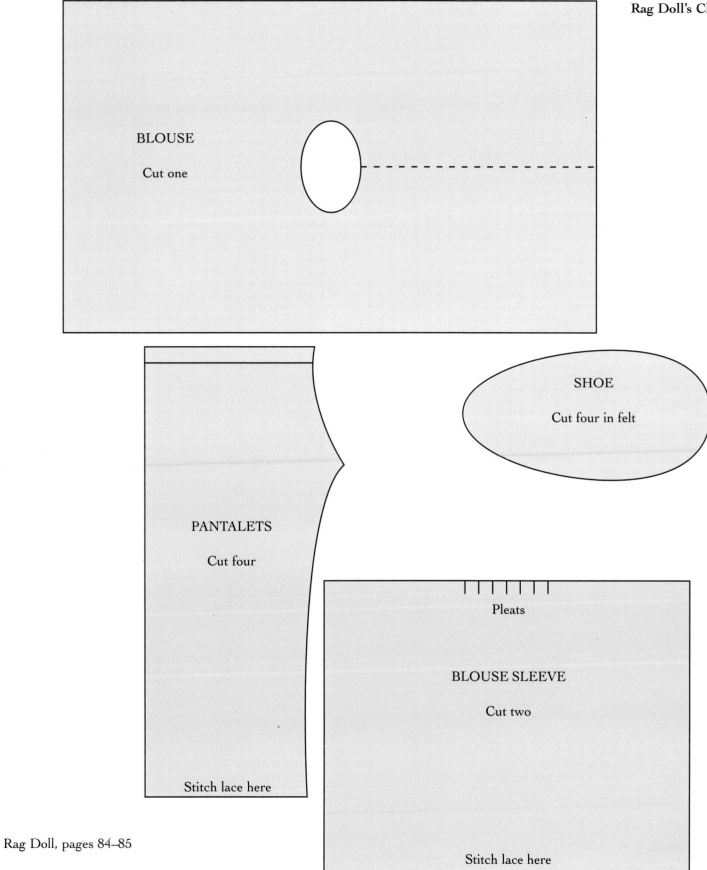

BLOUSE

Cut one

SHOE

Cut four in felt

PANTALETS

Cut four

Pleats

BLOUSE SLEEVE

Cut two

Stitch lace here

Stitch lace here

Rag Doll, pages 84–85

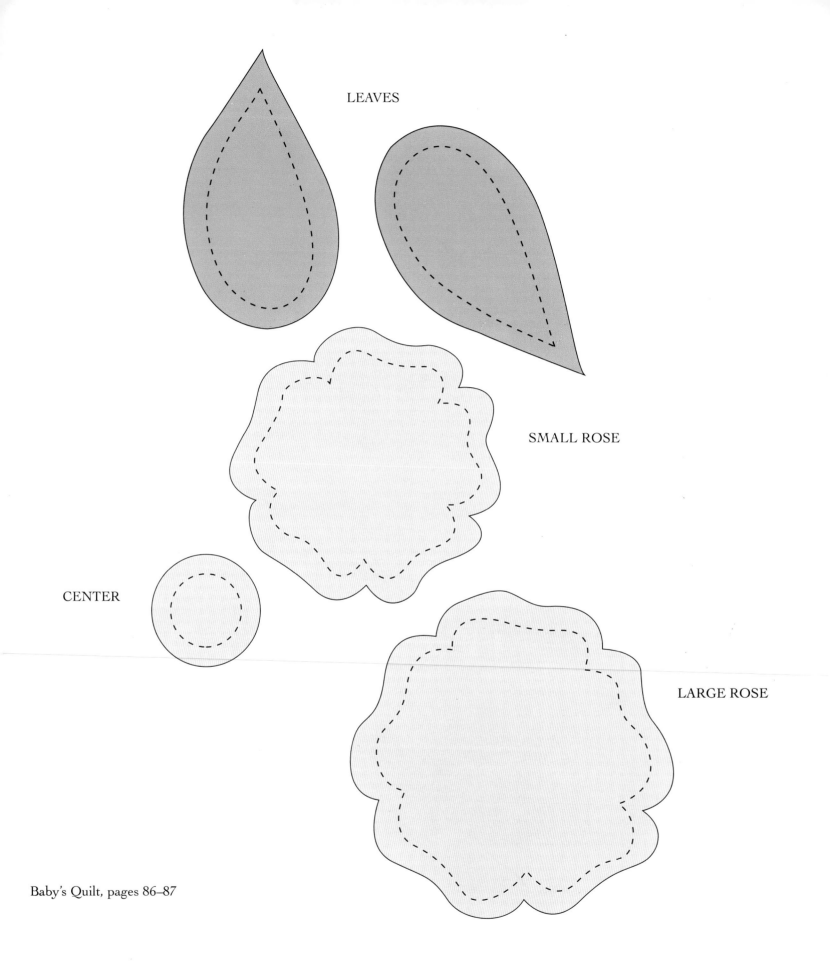

LEAVES

SMALL ROSE

CENTER

LARGE ROSE

Baby's Quilt, pages 86–87

Baby's Quilt, pages 86–87

- - - - - - - Quilting lines
Shaded areas indicate appliqué

ROOF

REINFORCING
STRIPS

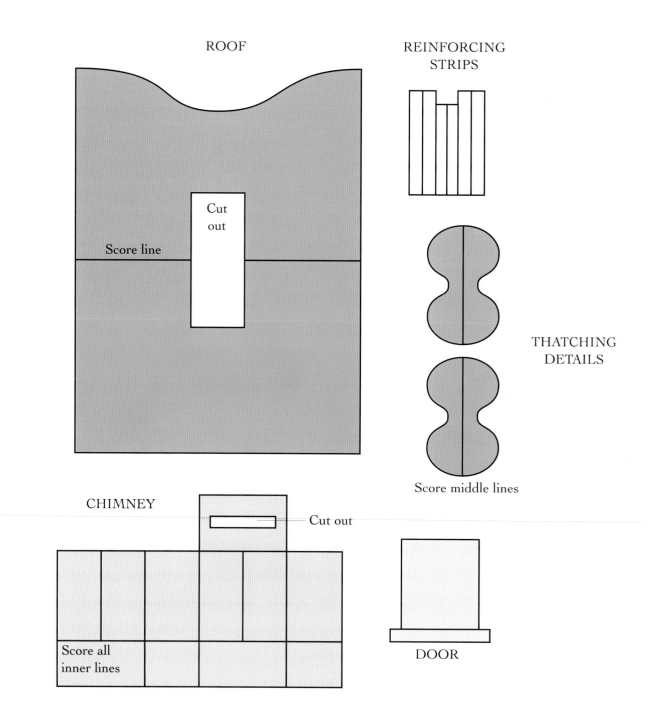

Cut
out

Score line

THATCHING
DETAILS

Score middle lines

CHIMNEY

Cut out

Score all
inner lines

DOOR

Cottage Coin Bank, pages 94–95

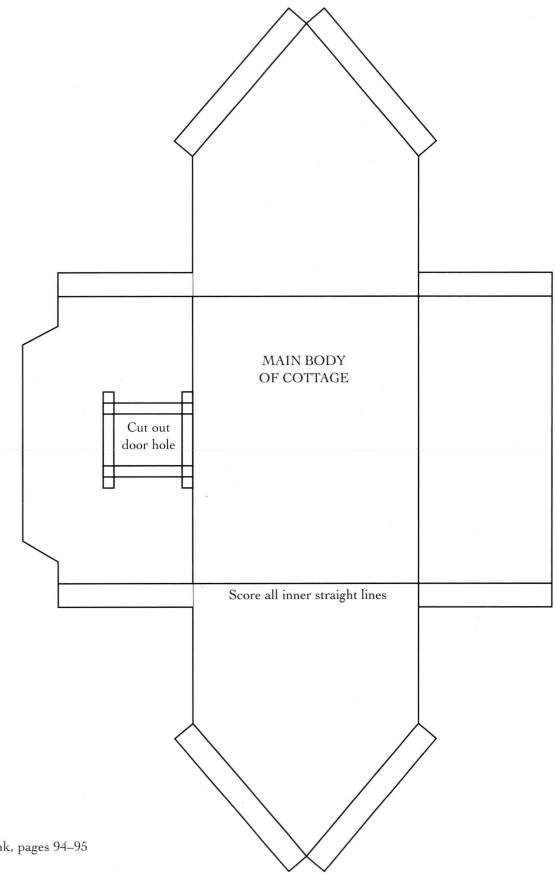

MAIN BODY
OF COTTAGE

Cut out
door hole

Score all inner straight lines

Cottage Coin Bank, pages 94–95

Suppliers

The author and the publishers would like to thank the following for their help in producing this book:

For supplying ribbons and roses:
C.M. Offray & Son Limited, Fir Tree Place, Church Road, Ashford, Middlesex TW15 2PH, United Kingdom

For details of stockists worldwide, the following outlets can be contacted:
C.M. Offray & Son Inc., Route 24, Box 601, Chester, NJ 07930-0601
(This address also applies to Australian customers.)

Ribbons & Roses, 8 Enkeldoring Street, Randpark Ridge Ext, 3, Randburg 2194, South Africa

For bear-making supplies:
The British Teddy Bear Association, P.O. Box 290, Brighton BN2 1DR, Great Britain

For supplying coton perlé and stranded floss:
DMC Creative World Limited, Pullman Road, Wigston, Leicestershire LE18 2DY, England

For details of stockists worldwide, the following outlets can be contacted:
The DMC Corporation, Port Kearny, Building 10, South Kearny NJ 07032, USA

S.A.T.C., 43 Somerset Road, P.O. Box 3868, Capetown 8000, South Africa

For supplying fusible interfacing:
Vilene Retail, Freudenberg Nonwovens L.P., Greetland, Halifax HX4 8NG
worldwide:
Freudenberg Pty Limited, P.O. Box 259, 3 Brand Drive, Thomastown, Victoria VO74, Australia

Freudenberg Nonwovens Limited, Chelmsford MA 01824, USA

For supplying gold embroidery thread, 002C Gold:
Kreinik Mfg Co.Inc., 9199 Reistertown Road, Ste 209B, Owings Mills, MD 21117, USA

Index

Acknowledgments

I would like to thank the editors, Jane Donovan and Samantha Gray,
who encouraged and helped me both professionally and personally.

The following friends designed and made heirlooms for the author:
Susan Gillespie of New Haven, MO, USA (the author's pen friend of many years)
for her Patchwork Quilted Pillows on pages 66–69 .
Pauline Brown for her granddaughter's Baby's Quilt on pages 86–87.
Shirley Salleh for her daughter's Tatted Collar on pages 78–81 .
Maria Kelly for her cross-stitch Wedding Sampler on pages 18–21.
Lizzie Cove for her Bears on pages 46–49.
Betty Fanning for her Victorian Pincushions on pages 34–37.
Lucy Griffiths for her Cottage Coin Bank on pages 94–95.
Garry Griffiths and Betty Fanning for the Garden Record Book on pages 30–33.
Juliet Bawden for the Christening Gown, Tea-Dyed Heart Pillow, and
Collage Memory Album on pages 24–27 and 44–45.
Barbara Stewart for her Gilded Frame on pages 54–55.
Jane Cook for her Hardanger Sachet on pages 38–41.

The following friends made up the author's designs:
Erika Brisland stitched the Tulip Sampler on pages 60–63.
Pauline Brown made the Rag Doll and the Wedding Album on pages 22–23.
Nikki Lutkin made the Plaid Sewing Basket and Needlecase on pages 74–77.
Garry Griffiths made the Recipe Book on pages 28–29.
The remaining designs were made by the author.